African Basin Management Organizations

International Water Law

Volumes published in this Brill Research Perspective are listed at *brill.com/rpwl*

African Basin Management Organizations

Contribution to Pollution Prevention of Transboundary Water Resources

By

Komlan Sangbana

BRILL

LEIDEN | BOSTON

This paperback book edition is simultaneously published as issue 5.1 of *International Water Law*,
DOI: 10.1163/23529369-12340017.

Library of Congress Control Number: 2020939191

Typeface for the Latin, Greek, and Cyrillic scripts: "Brill". See and download: brill.com/brill-typeface.

ISBN 978-90-04-43661-9 (paperback)
ISBN 978-90-04-43662-6 (e-book)

This book is printed on acid-free paper and produced in a sustainable manner.

Contents

To the memory of Professor Kader Asmal (1934–2011);
in recognition of his steadfast intellectual efforts in promoting
environmental protection in water governance.

African Basin Management Organizations

Contribution to Pollution Prevention of Transboundary Water Resources

*Komlan Sangbana**
Legal Officer, United Nations Economic Commission for Europe, Geneva, Switzerland
sangbana.komlan@gmail.com

Abstract

In Africa, basin organizations are almost indispensable mechanisms for any attempt to achieve the sustainable protection of transboundary water resources. Indeed, transboundary freshwater pollution is a growing concern at the African transboundary basin level. In this context, African basin organizations play a central role in the protection of transboundary water resources and their ecosystems. In order to prevent pollution damage and protect water resources, basin institutions have been entrusted with a variety of functions and tasks in the formation and implementation of pollution control standards. This monograph explores and highlights the increasingly important role of basin organizations in this area and provides some avenues for strengthening the work they perform to protect river systems.

Keywords

river basin organizations – pollution – Africa transboundary water resources – ecosystem – public participation – pollution control standards

* The views expressed herein are those of the author and do not necessarily represent the views of the United Nations.

 | DOI:10.1163/9789004436626_002

Introduction

Basin organizations are forums in which dialogue and action can be engaged.[1] In this respect, they play an important role in the overall system of protection of shared fresh waters. As observed by the International Court of Justice (ICJ), the establishment of basin organizations responds above all to the need for coordination between states in the adoption and implementation of the necessary measures to protect this precious resource from the negative impacts of human activities.[2] The importance of basins organizations and commissions in supporting and fostering transboundary cooperation is well recognized by African countries.[3]

In Africa, some basin organizations were established shortly after the emergence of newly independent states, which reflected a willingness and perceived need at the time to cooperate early on in order to manage shared water resources with neighbouring territories. This was the case with the Inter-State Committee established by the four Senegalese river basin states, namely Guinea, Mali, Mauritania and Senegal in 1963. It was replaced in 1968 by the Organization of the Riparian States of the Senegal River (OERS). While the Inter-State Committee was exclusively concerned with the cooperation between these four states in the exploitation of the basin's water resources, the OERS aimed at cooperation in a broader sense, as it encompassed economic, educational, cultural and social development within its scope. As mentioned by Godana, the OERS had an organizational structure which was remarkable for this period in Africa due to its establishment of a Conference

1 L. Boisson de Chazournes, '*Organismes et commissions de bassin: aspect de coopération régionale et règlement des différends*', in M. Kamga & M. M. Mbengue (eds), *L'Afrique et le droit international: Variations sur l'organisation internationale, Liber Amicorum en l'honneur de Raymond Ranjeva* (Paris: Pedone, 2013) 435–444, at 439.

2 International Court of Justice (ICJ), Case concerning Pulp Mills on the River Uruguay (Argentina v. Uruguay), Judgment, 20 April 2010, at 77, para 188.

3 In this regard, Africa notably the Sub-Sahara, is probably one of the most advanced regions in the world regarding transboundary water cooperation. This is apparent from the analysis of the first review of the Sustainable Development Goal (SDG) indicator 6.5.2 on transboundary water cooperation jointly carried out by the United Nations Economic Commission for Europe (UNECE) and the United Nations Education Scientific and Cultural Organization (UNESCO) in 2017 and 2018. Out of the 27 countries in sub-Saharan Africa that reported data for river and lake basins, 10 countries reported having operational arrangements in place for all their transboundary river and lake basins. Eight of the 12 countries in the Southern Africa Development Community (SADC) region that share transboundary rivers and lakes report that over 70 per cent of their transboundary river and lake basins are covered by operational arrangements. See UN Water, UNECE, and UNESCO, *Progress on Transboundary Water Cooperation: Global Baseline for SDG Indicator 6.5.2* (Paris: UNESCO, 2018), at 36.

of States, a Council of Ministers and an Executive Secretariat.[4] This organization was founded before the creation of the Senegal River Basin Development Organization (OMVS) in 1972.

Other examples of basin commissions being established after independence include the Lake Chad Basin Commission and the River Niger Commission, both established in 1964. These two commissions were political and technical institutions designed in the form of a single coordinating organization. They were both composed of members recruited for their recognized skills in water planning and management or resource development (there were nine River Niger Commissioners, one per state and eight Lake Chad Basin Commissioners, two per state). On 21 November 1980, the heads of state of the nine Niger Basin states (Burkina Faso, Benin, Cameroon, Chad, Côte d'Ivoire, Guinea, Mali, Niger, and Nigeria) concluded the Convention Creating the Niger Basin Authority (1980 Niger Basin Authority Convention). The Authority replaced the River Niger Commission (see Article 1(2) of the 1980 Niger Basin Authority Convention), created by the 1964 Agreement relating to the Niger River Commission and the Navigation and Transport on the River Niger (see Article 1(3) of the 1980 Niger Basin Authority Convention whereby 'the Authority inherits all the assets and assumes all the obligations of the River Niger Commission').

Other attempts to institutionalize basin governance included the establishment of the Kagera River Basin Organization between Burundi, Rwanda and Tanzania in 1977. On the Nile Basin, a draft treaty providing for a basin-wide Nile Basin Commission was submitted to the 28th Meeting of the informal Nile Technical Advisory Committee held in Cairo from 6 to 9 December 1977. This was in conformity with the decision taken by the Egyptian and Sudanese governments to attempt to enlarge the Permanent Joint Technical Committee to include all other Nile Basin states.[5] Although, this initial attempt did not work, ongoing discussions between the nine Nile riparian states to create such a regional framework led to the establishment on 22 February 1999 in Dar-es-Salam of a transitional institution (until negotiations were finalized and a permanent institution established) named the Nile Basin Initiative. It was able to bring together for the first time the 10 riparian states (Burundi,

4 A. B. Godana, *Africa's Shared Water Resources. Legal and Institutional Aspects of the Nile, Niger and Senegal River Systems* (London: Frances Pinter, 1985), at 275.

5 *Id*, at 264.

Democratic Republic of Congo, Egypt, Ethiopia, Kenya, Rwanda, South Sudan, Sudan, Tanzania, and Uganda).[6]

In the Southern African Development Community region, one of the major characteristics is the presence of a large number of transboundary rivers. Each country in this region shares at least one river basin with another country, except of course islands states (Mauritius and Seychelles). Therefore, the adoption of the Revised Protocol on Shared Watercourses in the Southern African Development Community in 2000 (SADC Revised Protocol) had a major impact on the institutionalization of those basin organizations in Southern Africa.[7] Indeed, the SADC Revised Protocol requires watercourse states to establish appropriate institutions such as watercourse commissions. This encouraged the establishment of the Orange-Senqu River Commission (between Botswana, Lesotho, Namibia, and South Africa),[8] the Lake Tanganyika Authority (between Burundi, Democratic Republic of Congo, Tanzania, and Zambia),[9] the Limpopo River Commission (between Botswana, Mozambique, South Africa, and Zimbabwe),[10] the Lake Victoria Basin Commission (between Kenya, Uganda, and Tanzania),[11] and the Zambezi Watercourse Commission (between Angola, Namibia, Botswana, Tanzania, Malawi, Zambia, Mozambique, and Zimbabwe).[12]

In the West and Central African regions, despite the lack of any operational regional framework such as the SADC Revised Protocol,[13] several basin

---

6 On the establishment of the Nile Basin Initiative, see S. M. A. Salman, '*The Nile Basin and its Changing Legal Contours*' in S. McCaffrey, C. Leb & R. T. Denoon, (eds), *Research Handbook on International Water Law* (Cheltenham: Edward Elgar, 2019) 379–396, at 388–390; Salman, S. M. A., '*The Nile Basin Cooperative Framework Agreement: A Peacefully Unfolding African Spring?*', 31:1 Water International (2013) 17–29.

7 On the development of the SADC legal regime, see S. M. A. Salman, '*Legal Regime for the Use and Protection of International Watercourse in the Southern African Region: Evolution and Context*', 41, Natural Resources Journal (2001) 981–1022.

8 Agreement Establishing the Orange-Senqu River Commission (2000) [Orange-Senqu River Commission Agreement].

9 Convention on the Sustainable Management of Lake Tanganyika (2003) [Lake Tanganyika Convention].

10 Agreement on the Establishment of the Limpopo Watercourse Commission (2003) [Limpopo Watercourse Commission Agreement].

11 Protocol for Sustainable Development of Lake Victoria Basin (2003) [Lake Victoria Basin Protocol].

12 Agreement Establishing the Zambezi Watercourse Commission (2004) [Zambezi Watercourse Commission Agreement].

13 In the West Africa region, a Draft Directive on Shared Water Resources Management in West Africa was examined by an expert group of the Economic Community of West African States (ECOWAS) on 3 May 2017. The Draft Directive still awaits submission to the ECOWAS Council of Ministers for formal approval in order to become binding

organizations have been created with the influence of the integrated water resources management concept.[14] In central Africa, among the newly established river basin organizations, mention can be made of the International Congo-Ubangi-Sangha Basin Commission (CICOS) which evolved from a narrow navigation mandate at its creation in 1999 to a dual mandate organization to support navigation and promote integrated water resources management in the Congo Basin in 2007 (between Angola, Cameroon, Central African Republic, Congo, Democratic Republic of Congo, and Gabon).[15] In West Africa, mention can be made of the Volta Basin Authority created in 2007[16] by the six riparian countries of the Volta Basin (namely Benin, Burkina Faso, Côte d'Ivoire, Ghana, Mali, and Togo). Further, the Mono Basin River Authority was recently established in 2014 between Togo and Benin.[17] There are also other ongoing initiatives to establish new basin organizations, such as the Comoé-Bia-Tanoé Basin Authority (between Côte d'Ivoire, Ghana, Mali, and Burkina Faso with the support of the Economic Community of West African states). This level of dynamism in the institutionalization of African river basins reflects the

on all ECOWAS members states. See Global Water Partnership West Africa, *ECOWAS discusses Draft Directive on Shared Water Resources Management in West Africa*, 9 June 2017, https://www.gwp.org/en/GWP-West-Africa/WE-ACT/News--Events/ecowas-discusses-draft-directive-on-shared-water-resources-management-in-west-africa/, accessed 21 January 2020. In the Central Africa region, on 22 December 2017, the Council of Ministers of the Economic Community of Central Africa States (ECCAS) approved the draft Convention for the prevention and peaceful resolution of conflicts related to the management of the shared water resources in Central Africa in Brazzaville. The Convention requires a formal adoption by the ECCAS heads of states which will enable the ratification process to be launched in ECCAS member states. See UNECE, *Central African countries approve regional convention on transboundary water cooperation with UNECE support*, 22 December 2017, https://www.unece.org/info/media/presscurrent-press-h/environment/2017/central-african-countries-approve-regional-convention-on-transboundary-water-cooperation-with-unece-support/doc.html, accessed 21 January 2020.

14 K. Sangbana, '*La gestion intégrée des ressources en eaux partagées et les organismes de bassin en Afrique: le cas de l'Autorité du Bassin du Niger et de l'Autorité de la Volta*', in *Actes du colloque de la Société française pour le droit international, L'eau en droit international* (Paris: Pedone, 2011) 235–244.

15 Addendum to the Agreement establishing a uniform river regime and creating CICOS (2007). See http://extwprlegs1.fao.org/docs/pdf/con144671.pdf, accessed 21 January 2020.

16 Convention on the status of the Volta River and the Establishment of the Volta River Basin Authority (2007) [Volta River Basin Authority Convention].

17 Convention on the Statutes of the Mono River (2014), which crosses both countries and the created the Mono River Basin Authority. See https://www.riob.org/pub/INBO-24/files/assets/basic-html/page19.html, accessed 21 January 2020.

widespread perception in Africa of basin organization's being the *par excellence* means to implement international water law.

The institutionalization of African river basins is also characterized by an overall trend of institutional proliferation. Indeed, there are as many institutional structures as there are transboundary basins. Therefore, any attempt to capture this trend requires a degree of classification. The legal status of basin organizations is a relevant criterion to assist with this classification.

The first category of institutional structures in African practice are intergovernmental organizations (or international organizations) as defined in Articles 2(i) of the 1969 Vienna Convention on the Law of Treaties and the 1986 Vienna Convention on the Law of Treaties between states and international organizations or between international organizations. Currently, there is an intergovernmental organization status attributed to all major African international basins.[18] For basins that were not originally accorded an intergovernmental organization status, following the dissolution of their original institutional structure, such an organization status was accorded to them, as in the case of the River Niger Commission. On the other hand, other basins are undergoing a transformation, as was the case with the International Lake Chad Basin Commission. Initially created as a purely technical and coordinating institution, this Commission was accorded a plenary body of state representatives at the highest level: a Conference of Heads of State.[19] Its status as an intergovernmental organization is therefore no longer in doubt given its composition and extended mandate.

The above-mentioned organizations are generally designed as 'development agencies' supporting the economic and social development of riparian countries. They are responsible for liaising with member states with a view to ensuring the efficient use of basin waters, addressing any issues on basin related activities, promoting cooperation between member states, and harmonizing and coordinating national development policies to ensure the development of a fair and balanced shared water resources policy. In turn, member states provide intergovernmental organizations with the general competence to create basin development policies, guide any basin activities or developments,

---

18 See the Revised Convention Creating the Niger Basin Authority (1987) [Niger Basin Authority Convention]; the Orange-Senqu River Commission Agreement (2000), *supra* note 8; the Lake Tanganyika Convention (2003), *supra* note 9; the Limpopo River Commission Agreement (2003); the Lake Victoria Basin Protocol (2003), *supra* note 11; the Zambezi Watercourse Commission Agreement (2004), *supra* note 12; Volta River Basin Authority Convention, *supra* note 16.

19 M. Kamto, '*Le droit international des ressources en eau continentales africaines*', 36:1, Annuaire français de droit international (1990) 843–911, at 893.

and regulate and control the use of the water resources. Their legal status also entitles them to enter into legal transactions such as holding property or having liabilities (such as a debt).

The second category of institutional structures that can be observed in African practice is the structure described by Maurice Kamto as the 'international public management agency'.[20] These institutions generally take the form of 'a specialized or public service agency with legal personality and financial autonomy created by two or more states or an inter-state institution, with the objective of developing and/or exploiting common resources with a view to providing services to states and possibly to individuals'.[21]

These entities are not accorded a broad mandate in integrated water resources management but are instead designed to manage sector specific activities, such as the development and management of hydro power schemes, and the delivery of specific services to riparian countries, such as the sale of energy. Thus, the Bamako Convention Concluded between Mali, Mauritania and Senegal Concerning the Legal Status of Common Works of 21 December 1978 (Bamako Convention) stipulates in Article 15 that the management of common works is entrusted to 'management agencies' placed under the supervision of the OMVS. Under Article 17, these agencies are defined as 'public interstate or semi-public interstate enterprises with legal personality and financial autonomy', having in particular the capacity to contract and to institute legal proceedings. To this date, the Bamako Convention has been supplemented by four additional agreements.

Indeed, in 1997, two further agreements established autonomous agencies responsible for the management and operation of two dam facilities: the Convention creating the Agency for the Management and Exploitation of Diama and the Convention creating the Agency for Energy Management of Manantali. In 2011, the Convention for the establishment of the Agency for the Development and Exploitation of Navigation on the Senegal River was adopted to improve navigation between the fluvial ports in Senegal and Mauritania; and in 2017, the four riparian states adopted the Convention creating the Upper

20 *Id*, at 895, unofficial translation of the French phrase '*établissement publics internationaux d'exploitation*'. See also H. T., Adam, *Les organismes internationaux spécialisés. Contribution à la théorie générale des établissements publics internationaux* (Paris: Librairie Générale de Droit et de Jurisprudence, 1957).

21 *Id*, unofficial translation of the French version: '*agence spécialisée ou de service public jouissant de la personnalité morale et de l'autonomie financière créé par deux ou plusieurs États ou une institution interétatique, ayant pour objectif d'aménager et/ou d'exploiter des ressources communes en vue de fournir des prestations aux États et éventuellement aux particuliers*'.

Basin Works Management Agency following Guinea's accession to the OMVS.[22] This Agency is in charge of developing the potential of the Upper Senegal River Basin, located in the Republic of Guinea.

The Komati Basin Water Authority is another example of an 'international public management agency'. It was formed in 1993 under the Treaty on the Development and Utilization of the Water Resources of the Komati River Basin. This Water Authority was established as a binational entity between the Kingdom of Eswatini (formerly known as Swaziland) and the Republic of South Africa to implement Phase 1 of the Komati River Basin Development Project. Phase 1 comprises the design, construction, operation and maintenance of the Driekoppies Dam in South Africa and the Maguga Dam in Eswatini.[23]

The third and final category of institutional structures, which are limited in practice, are joint technical committees. This type of body does not have an international legal personality but operates through national agencies, which provide the necessary technical and administrative support. An example is provided by the Tripartite Permanent Technical Committee established by an agreement between South Africa, Mozambique and Eswatini in 1983.[24] This Technical Committee provides assistance to watercourse states with the management of water flow on the Incomati and Maputo Rivers, especially during times of drought and flood.[25]

This research monograph will focus on the practice of basin organizations that are accorded international legal personality and a broad mandate in water resources management. This type of organization clearly prevails in African practice, and reflects the trend in international practice towards the harmonization of multifunctional and increasingly structured basin organizations.[26] The emergence of the principles of sustainable development, prevention, precaution and integrated water resources management calls for more extensive and better equipped institutional cooperation frameworks to ensure the necessary coordination of water resources management and protection measures. It is through this perspective that several framework conventions set

22 The OMVS did not include Guinea as a member until Guinea finally acceded to the OMVS in 2006.

23 Komati Basin Water Authority (KOBWA), https://www.kobwa.co.za/, accessed 21 January 2020.

24 Agreement between South Africa, Swaziland and Mozambique relative to the Establishment of a Tripartite Permanent Technical Committee regarding Rivers of Common Interest (1983).

25 *Id*, Art. 5.

26 See Boisson de Chazournes, *supra* note 1, at 439.

out the functions that these institutions can perform. In this regard, within the United Nations system, the 1992 Convention on the Protection and Use of Transboundary Watercourses and International Lakes (Water Convention) is particularly interesting, as it promotes a range of activities and functions that basin organizations can carry out to help prevent transboundary impacts.[27] Similarly at the regional level, in 2010, the Southern African Development Community issued a set of guidelines that provide basic guidance for strengthening river basin organizations and include guidance on areas such as establishment and development, funding and financing, stakeholder participation, and environmental management.[28]

Whilst there is a wide range of benefits that flow from the joint management and transboundary cooperation of water resources, focus will be particularly placed on the contribution that African basin organizations make to the prevention of pollution in transboundary fresh water by analysing the range of functions they perform to protect river systems and ensure their sustainable use. The contribution of basin organizations towards the protection of transboundary water resources will also be assessed by reviewing both the role of these bodies in the formation (Part 1) and implementation (Part 2) of pollution control standards.

Part 1: Role of Basin Organizations in the Formation of Pollution Control Standards

The study of the contribution of African river basin organizations in the formation of pollution control standards leads to a focus on the standard setting role of these bodies. The structural and norm-based arrangements that are linked to the decision-making processes that ultimately lead to the adoption of pollution control standards will therefore be examined. Whilst these arrangements are difficult to identify due to the sheer diversity of basin organizations,[29]

---

27 See in particular, Article 9.2 of the Convention on the Protection and Use of Transboundary Watercourses and International Lakes (1992) [Water Convention]. See also UNECE, *Principles for Effective Joint Bodies for Transboundary Water Cooperation* (New York and Geneva: United Nations, 2018).

28 For further information see SADC, *Water & Sanitation*, https://www.sadc.int/themes/infrastructure/water-sanitation/, accessed 16 March 2020.

29 Indeed, according to the regimes considered, basin organizations have specific profiles. Their status, institutional structure, functions and powers differ according to the particularities of each watercourse and the interests pursued by the riparian states.

two essential functions stand out. As a forum for facilitating and assisting its member states in the cooperation of transboundary water resources, a basin organization can promote pollution control standards (I). As it is independent from the community of states that compose it, basin organizations can also take decisions as an autonomous entity that are distinct from its member states. In this case, it becomes a pollution control standards setter (II).

1.1 Basin Organizations: Promoters of Pollution Control Standards

One of the classic mandates of African basin organizations is to provide support and assistance to riparian states in their cooperation efforts. In the context of combating the pollution of transboundary water resources, this mandate is mainly aimed at facilitating dialogue between parties in order to adopt preventative standards. Whilst any such dialogue was limited for a long time to state parties (A), there is now an increasing involvement of non-state actors (B).

1.1.1 *Facilitation of Dialogue amongst Member States*

In order to promote dialogue between parties, river basin organizations (a) make the necessary information available to parties to adopt measures and (b) create forums to facilitate dialogue and interaction between parties.

1.1.1.1 Provision of Information

The function of basin organizations as information providers is essentially translated in practice through the collection and exchange of information. The collection and exchange of information aims to facilitate the production and availability of information useful for decision-making. In this respect, it is traditionally one of the central responsibilities of basin organizations in terms of cooperation on transboundary water resources. This is reflected at the global level in the Water Convention, which mentions, amongst the other key functions of joint bodies established to prevent, control and reduce transboundary impact on transboundary water resources, the need to '(a) collect, compile and evaluate data in order to identify pollution sources likely to cause transboundary impact; ... [and] (c) draw up inventories and exchange information on the pollution sources'. Similarly, at the African regional level, the SADC Guidelines for Strengthening River Basin Organizations recommends that

See L. Caflisch, '*Règles générales du droit des cours d'eau internationaux*', in L. Caflisch. & Tunkin, G., *Recueil des cours/Académie de droit international* (1989) 9–225, at 196–197; Kamto, *supra* note 19, at 889–911.

such organizations should develop and maintain a database on environmental data and information in order to prevent, monitor and control pollution.[30] This provision is consistent with international practice.[31] In fact, the first river commissions set up to combat the pollution of transboundary water resources were often entrusted with study and research mandates to determine the pollution sources.

The emergence of environmental observatories within the framework of African basin organizations is indicative of the role that these bodies play in the collection and dissemination of information. Indeed, the objective of those observatories is to monitor and measure changes in the aquatic environment in order to inform decision-making bodies and develop a shared vision of the scale of these basins.[32] To this end, observatories are equipped with the skills to collect, analyse and disseminate information. The environmental observatory in the Senegal River basin provides a very good illustration of this mandate.[33] Initiated in 2000, this project, which is currently operational, has led to the development of an information and decision-making system. This system allows the publication of reports on the state of the environment in the Senegal River basin.[34] Such initiatives are also in place at the Niger Basin Authority (NBA), the Volta Basin Authority and the Lake Chad Basin Commission.[35]

---

30 SADC, *Guidelines for Strengthening River Basin Organisations: Environmental Management* (Gaborone: SADC Secretariat, 2010), at 5.

31 Water Convention, *supra* note 27, Art. 9.2. See also Protocol concerning the Establishment of an International Commission for the Protection of the Moselle (1961), Art. 2(a); Convention concerning the Protection of the Waters of Lake Geneva against Pollution (1962), Art. 3(a); Agreement concerning the International Commission for the Protection of the Rhine against Pollution (1963), Art. 2.1(a); Convention and Statutes relating to the Development of the Chad Basin (1964), Art. 9(b) [Chad Basin Convention]; Article 13 of the Convention establishing the Senegal River Development Organization (1972), Art. 13[Senegal River Organization Convention]; Agreement on Great Lakes Water Quality (1978), Art. 7; Niger Basin Authority Convention, *supra* note 18, Art. 9.7(a); Limpopo Watercourse Commission Agreement, *supra* note 10, Art. 7.2(d). See also J. Sohnle, *Le droit international des ressources en eau douce: solidarité contre souveraineté* (Paris: La documentation française, 2002), at 380.

32 International Network of Basin Organizations (INBO) et al, *The Handbook for Integrated Water Resources Management in Transboundary Basins of Rivers, Lakes and Aquifers* (INBO and GWP, 2012), at 58.

33 Since the institutional reform of the OMVS in 2010, the OMVS Environment Observatory has been integrated into the Directorate of Environment and Sustainable Development. See OMVS organigram: http://www.omvs.org/content/organigramme.

34 See Organization for the Development of the Senegal River, *Rapport annuel sur l'État de l'Environnement et des Ressources Naturelles du Bassin du Fleuve Sénégal* (2006).

35 See INBO, *supra* note 32, at 59.

Environmental observatories reveal an institutionalization in the collection and exchange of information systems that also suggests variability in the ways in which such systems are implemented in practice. In practice, in the domain of pollution control, the collection and exchange of information by basin organizations generally leads to study and research initiatives related to the ecological and chemical status of shared water resources. This function is therefore part of a largely scientific and technical mandate. Given this, the collection and exchange of information often takes the form of ongoing research programmes. In such cases, the basin organization will be responsible on a continuous basis for preparing and carrying out all of the necessary research to determine the nature, importance and origin of the pollution.[36] The research conducted will generate reports that the organization shares on a regular basis with member states (see, for example, the annual report on the state of environment issued by the OMVS).

In Africa's transboundary water practice, such research is carried out on an ad hoc basis, and whilst not currently widespread, merits further exploration. In general, research on a specific topic is conducted at the request of a member state, whereby the basin organization takes on a similar function to that of a fact-finding and investigative body. A good illustration of this can be found in North American practice. Indeed, Article 7.1(g) of the 1978 Great Lakes Water Quality Agreement assigns to the International Joint Commission between the United States of America and Canada (IJC), among other things, the responsibility to conduct 'investigations on matters related to the Great Lakes Basin Ecosystem, as the Parties may from time to time refer to the Commission'.[37] Any investigations implemented under this process generally result in the publication of a report setting out the investigation findings, together with recommended measures to be adopted to address any water quality problems that were identified during the investigations. In practice, this particular investigative function has been exercised several times by the IJC.[38]

The establishment of measuring stations also contributes to this investigative function through the collection and dissemination of water quality

36 See, for example, in European practice, Article 2(a) of the Protocol concerning the Establishment of an International Commission for the Protection of the Moselle (1961).

37 This provision was also included in the Great Lakes Water Quality Agreement (2012) [Great Lakes Agreement (2012)]. Under Article 7.1(f) of the 2012 Agreement, one of the IJC's responsibilities is 'investigating any subjects related to "the Great Lakes Basin Ecosystem that the Parties may refer to the Commission"'.

38 On the practice of the IJC, see in particular S. J. Toope & J. Brunnée, '*Freshwater Regimes: The Mandate of the International Joint Commission*', 15, Arizona Journal of International and Comparative Law (1998) 272–287.

information. Indeed, through such measurement systems, basin organizations ensure the ongoing monitoring and assessment of the water quality in order to provide a coherent overall picture of the ecological and chemical status of shared water resources.[39] The Niger basin provides a good example, where the scale of its water quality monitoring system represents one of the most significant pollution control projects to date.[40] This system, prescribed and approved by states,[41] makes it possible to acquire statistical data relating to the physico-chemical aspects of its general operation (general monitoring) and to characterize the impact of point and diffuse-source pollution on the basin (impact monitoring). Overall, this system consists of 164 stations, of which 134 are general monitoring stations (independently assessing the quality of any external pressure on the basin) and 30 are impact monitoring stations (assessing the effects of specific anthropogenic activities such as certain cities, industries and mines).

On the data collection process itself, data is, with some exceptions, collected by the states, which in turn send it on to the transboundary basin organization.[42] States therefore remain at the centre of the process of collecting and exchanging information; the institution therefore appears more like a facilitator of the transmission of data between states. In order to ensure the availability of information by institutions, it is important that they obtain reliable, current and relevant information when needed in a timely manner and in their required format.

In practice, it can be tempting for states not to cooperate, by refusing to provide data or by providing incomplete or understated data on the situation in their portion of shared waters. An interesting mechanism to address this risk was provided by two obligations included in the 2012 Great Lakes Water Quality Agreement. The first requires the parties to provide all available data or other information on the water quality of the Great Lakes when requested by the IJC.[43] The second recognizes the IJC's jurisdiction to 'verify independently such data and information through tests or other means as it deems

39 For examples of water quality monitoring programmes see UNECE, *Guide to Implementing the Water Convention* (New York and Geneva: United Nations, 2013) at 80–81.

40 Information gathered during the interviews with Mr. Robert Y. Dessouassi, Head of the Niger Basin Observatory, NBA, Niamey, 12–15 November 2012.

41 This system was validated during the regional workshop held in Niamey 4–6 May 2010 as reported in a document provided by the NBA directly to the author entitled *Proceedings of the Regional Workshop to Validate the Pre-final Report of the Study for the Establishment of a Water Quality Monitoring System in the Niger Basin*, Niamey, May 2010.

42 See INBO, *supra* note 32, at 51.

43 Great Lakes Agreement (2012), *supra* note 37, Art. 7.2.

appropriate'.[44] These provisions contribute significantly to ensuring that the basin organization is at the centre of the data collection and sharing process and can be further explored in African practice.

1.1.1.2 Creation of Consultation Forums

Consultation forums provide spaces for exchange and dialogue between riparian state representatives. By delivering such forums, basin organizations contribute to the maintenance of an important dialogue between riparian parties to help achieve the sustainable management of shared water resources. While these forums are essential for the protection of transboundary water resources from pollution, their form varies both in their structure and in their mode of organization.

Their structure generally consists of the periodic meeting of state representatives party to the basin organization. In practice, these bodies ensure that the state is represented at different levels. Three levels of representation can often be observed: (1) by heads of state and government; (2) by ministers; and (3) by senior officials appointed by their government. Some basin organizations provide for all three levels of representation. This is generally the case for intergovernmental organizations, such as the OMVS[45] or the Volta Basin Authority.[46] Other basin organizations provide only for the second and third levels of representation, or are limited to the third level of representation. This is the case for political and technical coordination institutions established in the Southern African Development Community such as the Permanent Okavango River Basin Water Commission[47] and the Orange Senqu River Commission,[48] which only provide for commissions composed of delegates from the contracting parties.

---

44 *Id*, Art. 7.1(a).

45 There is the Conference of the Heads of State and Government, the Council of Ministers, and the Standing Committee of Water as provided by Articles 3, 8 and 20 of the Senegal River Organization Convention, *supra* note 31.

46 There is the Assembly of Heads of State and Government, the Council of Ministers in Charge of Water Resources and the Committee of Experts as provided by Article 8 of the Convention on the Status of the Volta Basin Authority and Establishment of the Volta Basin Authority, 19 January 2007 (Benin, Burkina Faso, Cote d'Ivoire, Ghana, Mali, and Togo). See also A. Garané, *Le cadre juridique international du bassin de la Volta* (Gland: IUCN, 2009), at 249–256.

47 Agreement between the Governments of the Republic of Angola, the Republic of Botswana and the Republic of Namibia on the Establishment of a Permanent Okavango River Basin Water Commission (1994), Art. 2 [OKACOM Agreement].

48 Orange-Senqu River Commission Agreement, *supra* note 8, Art. 2.

In most cases, these bodies are provided for by the basin organization's relevant legal instruments; therefore, the forums are institutionalized *de jure*. However, institutionalization can also take place *de facto*. This is the case when the body in question has been created empirically. This can be observed in institutions that have at their core a predominantly technical function. The Lake Chad Basin Commission provides an illustration of this. The Lake Chad Basin Commission was originally created as a commission of eight experts with two from each of the four member states.[49] Subsequently, a Conference of the Heads of State and Government was set up without a written basis and met for the first time on 5 and 6 July 1972.[50]

The sessions of the various bodies described above provide a framework for the exchange of information and dialogue between the organization's member states. Such a degree of ongoing consultation helps to ensure an effective level of cooperation in pollution control matters. The meetings also contribute to the reinforcement of the organization's role as a governance tool for the prevention of pollution.

The organization of these forums varies in practice, and generally depends on the nature of the various basin organizations. In the case of political bodies, sessions are plenary. Where forums are institutionalized, the periodicity of such sessions is determined by the relevant legal instruments. The general tendency is to seek a balance between, on the one hand, maintaining a continuous dialogue between the parties and, on the other hand, ensuring that the regular holding of ordinary sessions does not become an obstacle for the parties.[51] As a general rule, the supreme organs of the institution (which are composed of heads of state and government or relevant ministers) meet less frequently. Heads of state and government may meet in ordinary session once a year or once every two years.[52] Ministers[53] may in some cases also meet in ordinary session once a year[54] and, in other cases, they meet on average twice

49 Chad Basin Convention, *supra* note 31, Art. 8.

50 See Kamto, *supra* note 19, at 893.

51 See *id*, at 903.

52 Senegal River Organization Convention, *supra* note 31, Art. 4; Convention relating to the Creation of the Gambia River Basin Development Organization (1978), Art. 5 [Gambia River Basin Organization Convention].

53 Niger Basin Authority Convention, *supra* note 18, Art. 6.4; Statutes of the Volta Basin Authority (2007), Art. 5.4 [Volta Basin Authority Statutes].

54 Niger Basin Authority Convention, *supra* note 18, Art. 7.3; Agreement on the Cooperation for the Sustainable Development of the Mekong River Basin (1995), Art. 17; Volta Basin Authority Statutes, *supra* note 53, Art. 6.9.

a year.[55] These organs may also convene extraordinary sessions depending on the circumstances.[56]

In the case of bodies with technical expertise such as commissions composed of senior government officials, the organization is somewhat different. The frequency of meetings depends on the nature of the organization. In the case of plenary organs, sessions are generally held annually, with the possibility of convening extraordinary sessions,[57] whereas in the case of smaller bodies, meetings are held more frequently.[58] The frequency of *de facto* forums is more difficult to assess because of the lack of a statutory base. Comparatively, for instance, sixteen sessions have been held by the International Commission for the Protection of the Rhine since 1950, with intervals of three to five years between the sessions held from 1994 to 2020.[59] However, the irregularity of this European basin organization's sessions is compensated by the existence of a regular dialogue between the state delegates under the Commission's plenary assembly framework.

1.1.2 *Facilitation of the Participation of Non-State Actors*

Taking into account the participation of non-state actors reflects a new form of governance based on their involvement in the decision-making of the management of transboundary water resources.[60] This participatory approach

55 Senegal River Organization Convention, *supra* note 31, Art. 10.1.

56 *Id*, Arts 4.1, 10.2; Gambia River Basin Organization Convention, *supra* note 52, Art. 10.1; Niger Basin Authority Convention, *supra* note 18, Arts 6.5, 7.4; Volta Basin Authority Statutes, *supra* note 53, Arts 5.5, 6.9.

57 This is the case of the meeting of the Permanent Okavango River Basin Water Commission which meets at least once per year in ordinary session. However 'more meetings may take place according to the need for such meetings'. See OKACOM Agreement, *supra* note 47, Art. 3.1.

58 For example, the Permanent Water Commission of the OMVS and the Gambia River Basin Development Commission meet as needed. See Senegal River Organization Convention, *supra* note 31, Art. 20; Gambia River Basin Organization Convention, *supra* note 52, Art. 19.

59 11th Conference of Ministers (8 December 1994); 12th Conference of Ministers (22 January 1998); 13th Conference of Ministers (29 January 2001); 14th Conference of Ministers (18 October 2007); 15th Conference of Ministers (28 October 2013); 16th Conference of Ministers (13 February 2020).

60 See K. M. Krchnak, '*Improving Water Governance Through Increased Public Access to Information and Participation*', 5:1, Sustainable Development Law and Policy (2005) 34–39; A. D. Ryabtsev, '*On Public Participation in Water Resources Management*', in P. Wouters, V. Dukhovny & A. Allan, (eds), *Implementing Integrated Water Resources Management in Central Asia* (Dordrecht: Springer, 2007) 89–94; J. Razzaque, '*Public Participation in Water Governance*', in J. W. Dellapenna & J. Gupta, (eds), *The Evolution of the Law and Politics of Water* (Dordrecht: Springer, 2009) 353–371; M. Tignino, '*Les contours du principe de la participation du public et la protection des ressources en eau transfrontières*', VertigO—la

echoes the concept of integrated water resources management. Integrated water resources management implies the involvement of all stakeholders and interested parties.[61] In practice, in African basin organizations, the public's involvement in the development of norms for the protection of transboundary water resources is facilitated by the establishment of institutional mechanisms for the representation of non-state actors. These unique representation mechanisms institutionalize the notion of public participation in transboundary water governance. The development of such mechanisms was in response to the need for the formal organization and representation of the various structural components of civil society in order to ensure their effective participation in the work of basin organizations.

The institutional representation mechanism can take the form of a statutory body of the basin organization. This is the case of the Forum of Stakeholders for the Development of the Volta Basin provided for in Article 8 of the 2007 Convention on the Status of the Volta River and Establishment of the Volta Basin Authority (Volta Basin Authority Convention).[62] According to the 2007 Statutes of the Volta Basin Authority, this Forum is 'an advisory body instituted by the Council [of Ministers]'.[63] It is made up of representatives of the various categories of water users, including civil society members involved with water resources management[64] and representatives from water and environmental sector research centres.[65] The main role of the Forum is to provide the Council of Ministers with the opinions and proposals of stakeholders in any basin

---

revue électronique en sciences de l'environnement (2010), http://vertigo.revues.org/9750 (accessed 22 January 2020); L. De Stefano & G. Schmidt, '*Public Participation and Water Management in the European Union: Experiences and Lessons Learned*', in B. Cosens, (ed), *The Columbia River Treaty Revisited: Transboundary River Governance in the Face of Uncertainty* (Corvallis: Oregon State University Press, 2012) 383–397; M. Tignino & K. Sangbana, (eds), *Public Participation and Water Resources Management: Where Do We Stand in International Law?* (Paris: UNESCO-IHP, 2015) p. 153; K. Sangbana, 'The Role of Non-State Actors in the Development and Implementation of International Water Law', in A. Rieu-Clarke, A. Allan & S. Hendry, (eds), *Routledge Handbook of Water Law and Policy* (Abingdon: Routledge, 2017) 287–296.

61 On basin commissions and integrated water resources management, see Sangbana, *supra* note 14, at 235–244.

62 See also Volta Basin Authority Statutes, *supra* note 53, Art. 4.3.

63 *Id*, Art. 7.1.

64 *Id*, Art. 7.2(a).

65 *Id*, Art. 7.2(d).

development,[66] including those related to pollution control.[67] As a permanent body, the Forum has its own internal rules and procedures.[68]

A similar representation mechanism can be found at the OMVS with the Senegal River Basin Committee. Established by the OMVS Council of Ministers in 2009,[69] this Committee is composed mainly of public and private actors from the basin area. Private actors include water and electricity utilities, agricultural organizations, transport operators, non-governmental organizations, customer associations and the scientific community.[70] Its primary role is to put forward, to the Council of Ministers, the main views in relation to the protection of the environment and the management of the environmental and social impacts flowing from the major structural developments included in the master plan for the development and management of the Senegal River's waters.[71]

The practice of the NBA also provides an example of this tendency to institutionalize the participation of non-state actors. Indeed, the need to involve civil society in the governance and protection of the Niger River Basin has been highlighted by NBA member states.[72] Civil society refers to 'all collective

---

66 *Id*, Art. 7.4.

67 Information gathered by the author during interviews with Mr. Charles Biney, Acting Executive Director of the Volta Basin Authority, Ouagadougou, 22 November 2012.

68 Volta Basin Authority Statutes, *supra* note 53, Art. 7.6.

69 Resolution No. 499 of the Senegal River Basin Committee, adopted at the 62nd Ordinary Session of the OMVS Council of Ministers, 22–23 October 2009, Nouakchott, Mauritania (unpublished document).

70 F. Bedredine & G. Fabre, '*Examples of concerted and supportive management of a shared river basin (Guinea, Mali, Mauritania, Senegal)*', paper presented at the International Network of Basin Organization, 10th World General Assembly, Dakar, Senegal, January 2010, at 10.

71 See Resolution No. 499, *supra* note 69.

72 Resolution No. 2 on the involvement of civil society in the shared vision process, 25th Ordinary Session of the NBA Council of Ministers, Niamey, 14 September 2006. A major point advocated by the 'Shared Vision' was the actual process leading to public involvement in decision-making. This was based on the NBA's invitation to regional organizations to take part in the regional validation workshop of the regional synthesis report of multi-sectoral studies. This workshop was held in Bamako from 25 to 29 January 2005. The report of this workshop noted 'the need to involve civil society in the Shared Vision process' and recommended that civil society adopt a 'common and consensual approach to take into account the concerns of all stakeholders in the basin'. See NBA, *Civil Society Implication*, http://www.abn.ne/index.php?option=com_content&view=category&layout=blog&id=15&Itemid=0&lang=en, accessed 22 January 2020. On public participation in the NBA, see R. Y. Dessouassi, '*État du processus de gestion intégrée des ressources en eau dans le Bassin du Niger: Expériences de l'implication des acteurs non étatiques et de la prévention des conflits entre usagers de ressources*', in M. Tignino and K. Sangbana, (eds),

actors "users of natural resources" in the River Niger Basin and who are active at local, national and regional levels in the basin according to their own formal or informal methods of organization and whose action or activity has a direct and/or indirect impact on the basin's natural, political and socio-economic environment'.[73] From this definition, two cumulative criteria can be found to identify non-state actors that are likely to be involved in basin management: (1) their activities must have a direct or indirect impact on the basin's natural, political and socio-economic environment; and (2) they must be organized in a formal or informal way.

Faced with the impossibility of involving all civil society actors in the work of NBA statutory bodies, a National Coordinating Unit of Users of the Niger River Basin's Natural Resources was therefore set up for each of the nine member states.[74] These nine coordinating units are in turn represented by a Regional Coordinating Unit of Users of the Niger River Basin's Natural Resources (RCU). The RCU is entitled to participate directly in formal NBA meetings.[75] Thus, the President of the RCU, in addition to being invited to all expert meetings and workshops, participates in the sessions of the Council of Ministers and the Summit of Heads of State.[76]

With respect to the Southern African Development Community, although the SADC Revised Protocol did not provide provisions on public participation, in 2010 it published guidelines for strengthening stakeholder participation within river basin organizations. According to these guidelines, stakeholder participation can be defined as 'the process of involving stakeholders in problem-solving or decision-making and using the stakeholders input to make better decisions'.[77] A stakeholder is also described as 'an individual, group or institution that has a defined and recognized interest, or stake, in a decision making process or project'. According to the guidelines, the elaboration of a participation framework is one of the key strategic areas that should be considered by river basin organizations 'aspiring to implement participatory processes'.[78] The Basin Wide Forum established by the Permanent Okavango

Public Participation and Water Resources Management: Where Do We Stand in International Law? (Paris: UNESCO-IHP, 2015) 69–76.

73 *Id*, NBA website.

74 See Dessouassi, *supra* note 72, at 74.

75 Information gathered during the author's interviews with Mr. Robert. Y. Dessouassi, Head of the Niger Basin Observatory and Mr. Barry Boubacar, Expert on Civil Society and National Focal Structures, NBA, Niamey, 12–15 November 2012.

76 *Id.*

77 SADC, *Guidelines for Strengthening River Basin Organisations: Stakeholder Participation* (Gaborone: SADC Secretariat, 2010), at 1.

78 *Id.*

River Basin Water Commission provides an example of a participation framework. This particular structure brings together groups such as tribal government representatives, community institutions (such as village development communities and village technical committees), as well as representatives from water user groups (particularly farmers, fishermen and craftsmen).[79] One of the essential functions of the Basin Wide Forum is to provide members with socio-economic and environmental information to facilitate the adoption of adequate standards of protection for the basin.[80]

It should be noted that these institutional mechanisms for public representation serve generally as platforms for public consultation. Public consultation is being increasingly promoted to allow the involvement of non-state actors in the policy development process and the formulation of regulation with respect to basin organizations. Such consultations appear as a process that allows basin organizations to collect views and proposals from the local community on issues relating to the management and protection of transboundary water resources. Public consultations can be observed in the practice of the OMVS. Local coordinating committees,[81] hosted by OMVS national units[82] in each member state, serve as excellent platforms for the participation of local communities because of their geographical mandates. By bringing together, amongst others, representatives of professional associations and local non-governmental organizations,[83] these committees have facilitated public consultation during the formation of the Water Development and Management Master Plan on the Senegal River. Similarly, the Basin Wide Forum set up under the framework of the Permanent Okavango River Basin Water Commission facilitates the holding of public consultations. Through these unique mechanisms of representation, the basin organizations examined demonstrate a desire to no longer appear only as organizations for the management and protection of international rivers, but also as development agencies for the benefit of the communities living in the river basin.

---

79 OKACOM, *Basin Wide Forum*, http://www.okacom.org/okacoms-work/partners-and-projects/partners/communities/basin-wide-forum, accessed 22 January 2020.

80 *Id.*

81 On Local Coordinating Committees, see M. Sow & B. Touré, *État des lieux du cadre juridique et institutionnel dans la région d'intervention en Mauritanie* (OMVS/GEF/BFS, 2008), at 6. Information is also available on the OMVS website, http://www.portail-omvs.org/participation-du-public/comites/comite-coordination-clc-cnc, accessed 22 January 2020.

82 The OMVS national units are in charge of coordinating OMVS activities in each member state. Information is available on the OMVS website: http://www.omvs.org/content/clc-cnc accessed 31 March 2020.

83 Bedredine & Fabre, *supra* note 70, at 10.

The granting of 'observer status' is another means used by some African basin organizations to involve non-state actors. This is the case with the Permanent Water Commission of the OMVS. According to Article 23 of the Senegal River Water Charter, observer status with the Permanent Water Commission may be granted to, amongst others, representatives of river users and non-governmental organizations. Such participation is, however, limited by the selection procedure. Observer status can only be granted by the decision of the Council of Ministers on the proposal of the OMVS High Commissioner.[84] Additionally, observer status candidates must be screened by the national authorities of each state party and proposed to the OMVS High Commissioner. Furthermore, in order to participate, the entity must be directly concerned with the relevant case before the Permanent Water Commission.[85] The immediate consequence of this participation mechanism is that the granting of observer status is temporary and restricted to meetings in which the observer's presence is relevant.

In addition, if observer status is granted, the right of an observer to intervene as a participant is restricted. For instance, the Rules and Procedures of the Permanent Okavango River Basin Water Commission consider an observer to be 'a person that ... has been allowed by the Co-Chairperson of the Commission at a particular meeting ... to listen to the discussions at the meeting that may be of interest to the observer or the institution that is represented by the observer'.[86] From this definition of an observer, the Rules and Procedures also stipulate that 'observers shall not be permitted to participate in the discussions at a Commission meeting unless specifically requested to do so by the Co-Chairperson'.[87] Observers essentially have the function 'to inform the Commission or to clarify some issues raised during the discussions at the meeting in connection with issues relevant to his or her presence in the meeting'.[88]

The practice of facilitating the participation of non-state actors through institutional mechanisms of public representation and observer status indicates an evolution in water governance in Africa. Consultation forums no longer therefore appear only as places for inter-state consultation, but as

84 Senegal River Water Charter (2002), Art. 23.

85 Information provided to the author by Mr. Malang Diatta, Expert in charge of the Secretariat of the OMVS Permanent Water Commission, Dakar, 20 November 2012.

86 Rules and Procedures of the Permanent Okavango River Basin Water Commission (2010), para 4.7.1. Available at http://www.okacom.org/site-documents/key-documents, accessed 22 January 2020.

87 *Id*, para 4.7.3.

88 *Id*, para 4.7.2.

'participatory forums' that bring together all the various actors concerned with the protection of transboundary water resources.

1.2 Basin Organizations as Standard Setters

There are many examples of the attribution of normative powers to contemporary basin organizations. This is due to the growing practice of entrusting these bodies with the task of defining the regulatory framework for the management and protection of transboundary basins and, consequently, the norms for the prevention, reduction and control of pollution. Through the production of norms, basin organizations contribute to the development of rules to combat pollution and promote the harmonization of such rules at the basin level. This part of the study focuses on acts relating to the protection and preservation of transboundary water resources. In this monograph, reference to 'instrument' means 'expressions of will of a general nature that set out rules of conduct in a written text, generally intended for the member states of the Organization, for the purpose of their conduct outside of the Organization'.[89] These are, therefore, all of the instruments which a basin organization uses in order to attempt to 'regulate' the conduct of their member states. In practice, the normative powers of African basin organizations to combat the pollution of transboundary water resources is exercised in various ways. However, the contours of this standard-setting function can be defined by reviewing its outward manifestations (A) and the methods in which it is exercised (B).

1.2.1 *Manifestations of the Normative Powers of Basin Organizations*

The normative powers of basin organizations are reflected by the adoption of different instruments of varying legal character. To regulate the conduct of member States, the African basin organizations have recourse to normative tools of a mandatory nature, such as water charters (a), appendices (b) and technical regulations (c), as well as normative tools of a recommendatory nature (d).

89 Unofficial translation of the French version '*manifestations de volonté de portée générale qui énoncent dans un texte écrit des règles de conduite, à l'intention généralement des États membres de l'Organisation, ayant pour objet leur comportement à l'extérieur de celle-ci*'. C. Dominicé, '*Valeur et autorité des actes des organisations internationales*', in R.-J. Dupuy, (ed), *Manuel sur les organisations internationales* (2nd edition, Dordrecht: Martinus Nijhoff, 1998) 441–484, at 441.

1.2.1.1 Water Charters in Africa and Pollution Control

In African practice the adoption of 'water charters' by basin organizations demonstrates their use of conventions as a way of expressing their normative powers.[90] Indeed, as pointed out by Makane Moïse Mbengue, these charters are treaties, subject to the law of treaties, and are therefore codified in some respects by the Vienna Conventions on the Law of Treaties.[91]

The charters are used by African institutions as a regional policy tool in the management of shared water resources, that is, policy instruments that are at their disposal in the management and protection of the basin. In many ways, this approach is linked to the function accorded to the relevant institution, namely that of the development of the basin.

The process of adopting the Niger Basin Water Charter in 2008 provides an example. Indeed, this instrument is presented as one of the principal results arising from the negotiation of the 'Shared Vision' initiated and developed within the framework of the NBA.[92] The Shared Vision consists of a comprehensive plan for the development of the basin, negotiated and approved by all member states and other stakeholders and users of the basin resources.[93] Its objectives are as follows:

> developing water resources in a sustainable and fair way so as to promote prosperity, security and peace between the populations of the River Niger Basin;
>
> strengthening the existing legal and institutional framework promoting dialogue and concerted action for co-operation amongst the NBA Member States; and
>
> developing on a participatory and consensual basis, a strategic framework for integrated development—the Sustainable Development Action

90 On water charters, see M. M. Mbengue, '*Les Chartes de l'eau: vers une nouvelle conception de la gestion des ressources en eau partagées en Afrique ?*', in M. Kamga & M. M. Mbengue, (eds), *L'Afrique et le droit international: Variations sur l'organisation internationale, Liber Amicorum Raymond Ranjeva* (Paris: Pedone, 2013) 219–231; M. Ngaïde, '*La contribution de l'Afrique à la gestion des ressources en eau transfrontalières: l'exemple de la Charte de l'eau du Bassin du Niger*', 66, Revue juridique et politique des états francophones (2012) 263–316.

91 See Mbengue, *id*, at 226.

92 See Dessouassi, *supra* note 72, at 72.

93 C. Brachet and R. Dessouassi, *A Shared Vision for the Niger Basin* (Niamey: NBA, 2008), at 13, available at https://docplayer.fr/25264153-La-vision-partagee-du-bassin-du-niger-a-shared-vision-for-the-river-niger-basin-bassin-du-niger.html, accessed 22 January 2020.

> Plan (SDAP) [for the River Niger Basin]—and implementing it throughout the basin.[94]

Pollution control is one of the elements taken into account to ensure the effectiveness of the measures that are adopted as part of the realization of the Shared Vision.[95]

The Niger Basin Water Charter is an essential tool to ensure the implementation of the NBA's Shared Vision. In fact, its adoption applies Principle One of the Paris Declaration on the Principles of Good Governance and Management for Sustainable and Shared Development of the Niger Basin, which was adopted on 26 April 2004 by the NBA's Heads of State and Government Summit. In particular, this principle recommends that member states implement the Shared Vision for the development of the basin and 'to this end, they shall cooperate on a basis of solidarity and reciprocity, taking into account previous agreements and by means of new agreements, with a view to developing and implementing policies, programs and projects initiated in all or part of the basin'.[96] This provision allows the basin organization's member states to use conventional techniques in order to implement the basin's sustainable development policy. As highlighted in its preamble, the Charter's adoption is a concrete realization of this provision.[97]

Unlike the traditional instruments that tend to exclusively govern cooperation in an African river basin, charters have the particularity of appearing above all as instruments for the protection of shared water resources.[98] The choice of semantics is revealing: reference is made to 'water charter' and not 'water use charter'. Indeed, these charters are based on the universal rules and principles of international water law as codified mainly by the 1997 Convention on the Law of the Non-Navigational Uses of International Watercourses (Watercourses Convention), the Water Convention, as well as by the 2008 Articles on the Law of Transboundary Aquifers. In this respect, the charters contribute to the integration of African international law on shared water resources into

94 *Id*, at 16.

95 See in particular, Niger Basin Authority, *Elaboration du plan d'action de développement durable du bassin du Niger: Phase II: Schéma directeur d'aménagement et de gestion* (Niamey: NBA, July 2007), http://www.abn.ne/images/documents/textes/padd/phase_2_fr.pdf, in particular Abstract 22, p. 36.

96 Paris Declaration on the Principles of Good Governance and Management for Sustainable and Shared Development of the Niger Basin (2004).

97 See the Preamble to the Niger Basin Water Charter (2008): 'Determined to implement the Paris Declaration on the principles of management and good governance for the sustainable and shared development of the Niger Basin dated 26 April 2004'.

98 See Mbengue, *supra* note 90, at 227.

the universal perspective of the sustainable management of these resources and, consequently, to the development of the universal regime on the management of shared water resources.[99] By way of example, the Lake Chad Basin Water Charter expresses in its preamble its desire to contribute to efforts to 'progress towards a universal agreement on transboundary aquifers'.[100]

Amongst the universal norms of sustainable management included in water charters are those developed for pollution control. In the wake of the Watercourses Convention, the Senegal River Water Charter, which was the first in a series of charters, addresses the issue of pollution through the protection and preservation of the environment. Article 16 of the Senegal River Water Charter requires the parties to take 'provisions likely to prevent, reduce or control the events or conditions resulting from natural causes or human activities which are likely to cause a damage in the other states, the river environment, human health or safety'.

The Niger Basin Water Charter[101] and the Lake Chad Basin Water Charter[102] also impose an obligation on the parties to prevent pollution. However, with respect to the Niger Basin Water Charter, the concrete measures to combat pollution are detailed in Appendix 1 of the Charter which relates to the protection of the environment (Niger Basin Appendix on Environmental Protection).[103] The adoption of this Appendix, without having to go through the more traditional and conventional procedures, highlights the capacity that basin organizations have to produce other forms of binding instruments for their members.

Indeed, other than treaties, for the purpose of standard setting, the use by basin organizations of other binding instruments is not very widespread. In general, states are reluctant to transfer to international institutions the power to impose substantive obligations on them.[104] However, in the context of African basin organizations, such techniques have the advantage of bypassing the cumbersomeness of the conventional process to ensure the rapid adoption of technical instruments, which in turn facilitates the management and protection of shared water resources.

99 *Id.*

100 Water Charter for the Lake Chad Basin (2012), preamble [Lake Chad Basin Water Charter].

101 Niger Basin Water Charter, *supra* note 97, Art. 12.

102 Lake Chad Basin Water Charter, *supra* note 100, Arts 21–27.

103 Niger Basin Water Charter, Appendix 1, Chapter 4 relating to the Protection of Environment (2011) [Niger Basin Appendix on Environmental Protection].

104 G. Ulfstein, '*Les activités normatives de l'organisation internationale*', in E. Lagrange & J.-M. Sorel, (eds), *Traité de droit des organisations internationales* (Paris: LGDJ, 2013) 737–755.

1.2.1.2 Appendices

In treaty practice, appendices (or annexes) are provided in order to complement specific technical aspects of the principal treaty instrument. In certain cases, the primary mandate to adopt appendices is granted to basin organizations.[105] This is the case in the Niger basin where Article 33 of the Niger Basin Water Charter provides that 'the Charter may envisage appendices dealing with technical, financial or administrative matters'.

On the basis of Article 33, the NBA adopted, after the entry into force of the Niger Basin Water Charter on the 1 October 2011, the Niger Basin Appendix on Environmental Protection. According to the first paragraph of Article 2 of the Appendix, its purpose is, *inter alia*, 'to ensure adequate protection of the environment of the basin on the basis of sustainable, collaborative and participatory management of the environment in accordance with the goals of sustainable development'. The second paragraph of Article 2 also emphasizes that it 'clarifies and supplements the relevant provisions of the Charter' on environmental protection. In view of both its detailed content and broad scope (which encompasses all environmental sectors and natural resources in the basin), this Appendix constitutes an important instrument in the protection of the Niger basin's environment.

Although the Niger Basin Appendix on Environmental Protection acquires treaty value by virtue of its attachment to the Niger Basin Water Charter, it is unique in its mode of entry into force. Indeed, according to Article 229, it enters into force as soon as it is adopted by the NBA Council of Ministers.[106] Amendments to the Appendix are also subject to these same entry in force procedures.[107] It should be noted that the ability for an organ of a basin organization to adopt directly enforceable instruments is peculiar. It demonstrates the will of the parties to avoid the burdens that can accompany the traditional treaty process and to place the basin organization at the very heart of their shared basin's protection framework. However, this is not an inherent power. Rather, it is exercised on the basis of an express delegation of authority stipulated in the basic treaty instrument. Thus, the ability of the NBA Council of Ministers to adopt annexes is specifically provided for in Article 33 of the Niger

105 Any such basin organization's appendices are distinct from any appendices adopted by states. In such cases, instruments are subject to the same regime for their adoption and entry into force as the principal agreements to which they are appended.

106 The Council of Ministers is one of the four permanent bodies of the NBA. See Niger Basin Authority Convention, *supra* note 18, Art. 5.

107 Article 227.4 of the Niger Basin Appendix on Environmental Protection, *supra* note 103, reads as follows: 'Any amendment to this Appendix shall come into force under the same conditions as the Appendix'.

Basin Water Charter.[108] Similarly, Article 97 of the Lake Chad Basin Water Charter provides that the revision of all appendices prepared after the entry into force of the Charter shall be subsequently adopted by the Council of Ministers. In addition, Article 97 adds that 'Appendices adopted or revised by the Council of Ministers shall come into force thirty days after being adopted'.[109] Nevertheless, the adoption procedure, teamed with the absence of a ratification requirement, gives these institutions a real ability to set standards of conduct on its member states.

In some cases, the ability of basin organizations to generate new rules is more apparent when revising the appendices to the main treaty. This is the case in European practice with the International Commission for the Protection of the Danube River. Indeed, the Convention on Cooperation for the Protection and Sustainable Use of the Danube River adopted in 1994 (Danube River Convention), includes one main legal instrument and five annexes. Article 23(6) of the Convention gives the International Commission the power to amend Annexes I, II and III, in accordance with Article 5 of Annex IV (Statute of the International Commission for the Protection of the Danube River). This article sets out rules on the adoption of decisions at the Commission level. In particular, it specifies that once the decision has been adopted by the International Commission, it becomes 'binding on the first day of the eleventh month following the date of its adoption for all Contracting Parties that voted for it'.[110] The ability of the International Commission to adopt rules is all the more remarkable as it appears alongside other provisions that refer to the conventional treaty procedure.[111]

The assignment to basin organizations of the power to amend treaty appendices, and consequently to create norms, demonstrates the important role played by basin organizations in countering pollution. However, it should be stressed that the binding and enforceable nature of these standard setting decisions is generally diluted by an 'opt out' clause that preserves the sovereignty of

108 Article 33 of the Niger Basin Water Charter, *supra* note 97, reads as follows: 'The Charter may envisage annexes dealing with technical, financial or administrative matters. Such annexes shall enter into force after their adoption by the Council of Ministers'.

109 Lake Chad Basin Water Charter, *supra* note 100, Art. 97.

110 Convention on Cooperation for the Protection and Sustainable Use of the Danube River (1994), Annex 4, Art. 5.2 [Danube River Convention].

111 For example, under Articles 23.4 and 23.4, the entry into force of amendments to the main Danube River Convention is subject to ratification, acceptance or approval.

member states.[112] Thus, in general, such decisions are enforceable but subject to the risk of non-acceptance by any individual party.[113]

1.2.1.3 Technical Regulations

The adoption of technical regulations by basin organizations is an emerging trend in some African basins. This trend is based on the parties' desire for their measures to be coordinated through the basin organization. The materialization of this will to coordinate measures through the basin organization in the form of an obligation under the principal treaty explains the mandatory nature of these regulations, as emphasized by the ICJ in the case concerning *Pulp Mills on the River Uruguay*.

Indeed, Article 56 of the 1975 Statute of the River Uruguay entrusts the Uruguay River Administrative Commission (CARU) with the function of drawing up '*inter alia*, rules governing ... [the] prevention of pollution'. On the basis of this article, CARU adopted standards on the uses of the Uruguay River waters, which are found in the CARU Digest. The Digest mainly sets standards for water quality, by setting general limits for certain discharges or effluents from industrial installations, such as 'hydrocarbons', 'sedimentable solids' and 'oils and greases'.[114] The ICJ noted that the adoption of these technical regulations constituted an application of Article 36 of the Statute of the River Uruguay, which requires the parties to coordinate 'through the Commission, the necessary measures to avoid any change in the ecological balance and to control pests and other harmful factors in the river and the areas by it'.[115] The

112 On the 'opting out' technique see H. G. Schermers & N. M. Blokker, *International Institutional Law* (5th edition, Leiden/Boston: Martinus Nijhoff, 2011), at 808–809; M. M. Mbengue, '*Technique de l'opting out: acceptation par les États des normes techniques internationales*', in E. Brosset & E. Truilhé-Marengo, (eds), *Les enjeux de la normalisation technique internationale—Entre environnement, santé et commerce international* (Aix-en-Provence/Paris: CERIC/ La documentation française, 2006) 121–152; Ulfstein, *supra* note 104, at 748–749.

113 See, in particular, Danube River Convention, *supra* note 110, Annex 4, Art. 5.2; see also, Ulfstein, *supra* note 104, at 748–749.

114 See Pulp Mills Judgment, *supra* note 2, at 70, para 199.

115 *Id*, at 66, paras 183–184: '[183.] It is recalled that Article 36 provides that "[t]he parties shall co- ordinate, through the Commission, the necessary measures to avoid any change in the ecological balance and to control pests and other harmful factors in the river and the areas affected by it". [184.] It is the opinion of the Court that compliance with this obligation cannot be expected to come through the individual action of either Party, acting on its own. Its implementation requires co-ordination through the Commission. It reflects the common interest dimension of the 1975 Statute and expresses one of the purposes for the establishment of the joint machinery which is to co-ordinate the actions and measures taken by the Parties for the sustainable management and environmental protection

CARU Digest implements CARU's obligation to coordinate measures. As such, it reflects 'the will of the Parties and their interpretation of the provisions of the 1975 Statute' and helps to define more precisely and give more specific content to the general obligations to prevent, reduce and control pollution.[116] However, in the ICJ's view, the measures taken in compliance with the obligation to coordinate measures within the CARU framework 'consist not only in the adoption of a regulatory framework, as has been done by the Parties through CARU, but also in the observance as well as enforcement by both Parties of the measures adopted'.[117] Both parties are therefore obliged to implement the Digest adopted by CARU. Also, through the use of technical regulations, the regulatory action of basin organizations is more evident in that these bodies can regulate various areas of member state activity for the protection of shared water resources.

The ability to adopt technical regulations is within the mandate of several African basin organizations. For example, at the NBA, the Niger Basin Appendix on Environmental Protection stipulates that the responsibility to protect the environment falls jointly to the Executive Secretariat of the NBA, member states and national public authorities (Article 8). Within the framework of these prerogatives, Article 53 of the Niger Basin Appendix on Environmental Protection provides that state parties

(a) set goals and criteria for environmental quality;
(b) establish techniques and practices in the fight against pollution at source; and
(c) establish the list of substances whose introduction into the waters of the basin is prohibited, limited or submitted to researches or inspections.[118]

On the basis of this provision, at the NBA, work is currently in progress to adopt a set of technical regulations.[119]

---

of the river. The Parties have indeed adopted such measures through the promulgation of standards by CARU. These standards are to be found in Sections E3 and E4 of the CARU Digest'.

116 *Id*, at 70, para 199.

117 *Id*, at 66, para 185: 'In the view of the Court, the purpose of Article 36 of the 1975 Statute is to prevent any transboundary pollution liable to change the ecological balance of the river by co-ordinating, through CARU, the adoption of the necessary measures. It thus imposes an obligation on both States to take positive steps to avoid changes in the ecological balance. These steps consist not only in the adoption of a regulatory framework, as has been done by the Parties through CARU, but also in the observance as well as enforcement by both Parties of the measures adopted'.

118 See also Lake Chad Basin Water Charter, *supra* note 100, Art. 23: 'In cooperation with the State Parties, the Commission shall set standards for pollutant discharge'.

119 Interview with Dessouassi, *supra* note 40.

1.2.1.4 Soft Law Instruments

The standard setting powers of basin organizations may also include the adoption of 'soft law' instruments.[120] These instruments are not intended to 'regulate' the action of states, but rather to 'guide' them. Basin organizations, especially those with technical expertise, frequently use recommendations as a standard setting tool. The term 'recommendation' is a generic term used to refer to instruments that invite recipients to adopt a specific behaviour either by action or omission.[121] In fact, issuing recommendations is generally one of the main activities of basin organizations.

For example, Article 1.2 of the 1994 Agreement on the Establishment of a Permanent Okavango River Basin Water Commission states that '[t]he objective of the Commission shall be to act as technical advisor to the Contracting Parties on matters relating to the conservation, development and utilization of water resources of common interest to the Contracting Parties'. In this respect, this Agreement provides that the Commission's main function is to assist the parties by providing them with advice and recommendations on issues relating to the management and protection of the basin,[122] such as 'the prevention of the pollution of water resources and the control over aquatic weeds in the Okavango River Basin'.[123] Similar provisions are found in the Agreements establishing the Limpopo Watercourse Commission[124] and the Orange-Senqu River Commission.[125]

The use by basin organizations of recommendations as a means of expression is mainly due to their lack of binding force.[126] However, recommendations do retain some legal relevance as a tool to guide member states in the implementation of their international obligations to tackle pollution.

---

120 On the role of soft law in international law, see in particular, G. Abi-Saab, '*Éloge du "droit assourdi": quelques réflexions sur le rôle de la soft law en droit international contemporain*', in *Nouveaux itinéraires en droit: Hommage à François Rigaux* (Brussels: Bruylant, 1993), 59–68.

121 M. Virally, '*La valeur juridique des recommandations des organisations internationales*', 2, Annuaire français de droit international (1956), 66–96, at 68; J. Salmon, *Dictionnaire de droit international public* (Brussels: Bruylant, 2001), at 937. On recommendations, see also Schermers & Blokker, *supra* note 112, at 767–792; Dominicé, *supra* note 89; R. Higgins, '*The Role of Resolutions of International Organizations in the Process of Creating Norms in the International System*', in W. E. Butler, (ed), *International Law and the International System* (Dordrecht: Martinus Nijhoff, 1987) 21–30.

122 OKACOM Agreement, *supra* note 47, Art. 4.

123 *Id*, Art. 4.5.

124 Limpopo Watercourse Commission Agreement, *supra* note 10, Arts 3.1, 7.

125 Orange-Senqu River Commission Agreement, *supra* note 8, Arts 4, 5.

126 See Schermers & Blokker, *supra* note 112, at 767, para 1217.

At the outset, it should be noted that the flexibility of recommendations facilitates the acceptance and implementation by states of pollution control standards. Indeed, in an environment marked by a continuous incentive for states to cooperate, it can be preferable to adopt a recommendation that allows basin organizations to insert binding rules into a soft instrument. Once recommended, the standards can be incorporated into the domestic laws of states and become binding. Such an approach is much more effective than the adoption of binding instruments that are difficult to implement.

Moreover, although the very nature of a soft law instrument excludes their having a binding effect, the fact remains that their implementation or non-implementation may have legal consequences. Indeed, a riparian state that complies with the recommendations issued by a basin organization of which it is a member, is simply assuming the obligations it took on when it joined. It is about cooperating in relation to the parties shared resource, and taking into account the recommendations of the mechanisms put in place to facilitate this cooperation. To this end, some basin organizations impose an obligation on members to justify any refusal to follow the recommendation. This solution was foreseen in the framework of the International Commission for the Protection of the Rhine. Although the Convention on the Protection of the Rhine emphasizes the recommendatory nature of these decisions to the parties,[127] it imposes an obligation on the parties to provide regular reports to the Commission.[128] But above all, it provides in Article 11.4 that '[i]f a Contracting Party cannot implement the Commission's decisions, in full or in part, it shall report this within a specific time limit set by the Commission on a case-by-case basis and shall give its reasons'. As René-Jean Dupuy pointed out, the requirement to justify the refusal to implement an international body's recommendation is indicative of the exercise of regulatory power.[129] Thus,

127 See Article 11.1 of the Convention on the Protection of the Rhine (1999): 'The Commission shall communicate to the Contracting Parties, in the form of recommendations, its decisions on the measures referred to in Article 8(1)(b), which shall be implemented in accordance with the national law of the Contracting Parties'.

128 See Article 11.3 of the Convention on the Protection of the Rhine, *id*,: 'The Contracting Parties shall report regularly to the Commission on:
(a) the legislative, regulatory and other measures they have taken with a view to implementing the provisions of this Convention and on the basis of the Commission's decisions;
(b) the results of the measures implemented in accordance with subparagraph (a);
(c) the problems arising from the implementation of the measures referred to in subparagraph (a)'.

129 R.-J. Dupuy, '*État et organisation internationale /The State and International Organization*', in R.-J. Dupuy (ed), *Manuel sur les organisations internationales / A Handbook on International Organizations* (2nd edition, Dordrecht: Martinus Nijhoff, 1998), at 25.

through this obligation to justify, the legal force of the recommendations of the International Commission for the Protection of the Rhine are strengthened and their non-binding nature somewhat diluted.

The question may be raised as to whether the duty of justification must necessarily result from an explicit reference in a treaty text. In the author's opinion, it is not essential to always have such a treaty foundation. The duty of justification is inherent in granting the power to make recommendations. A parallel can be drawn with the ICJ's Advisory Opinion in the case concerning the *Voting Procedure on Questions Relating to Reports and Petitions Concerning the Territory of South-West Africa* in respect of the resolutions of the United Nations General Assembly. Although this Advisory Opinion does not concern a basin organization and relates to a body with much wider-ranging powers, the ICJ sets out criteria that can be applied to basin organizations. In this Advisory Opinion, the ICJ held that the powers of the United Nations General Assembly to receive and examine the annual reports relating to the territory of South-West Africa derived from Article 10 of the 1945 Charter of the United Nations (which authorizes it to discuss any questions or cases falling within the scope of the Charter, and make recommendations to the members of the United Nations on such questions or cases).[130] Applying this very reasoning to this study, the power of basin organizations to receive and examine reports from riparian states could emerge, without any treaty basis, from their power to define the regulatory framework in respect of the management and protection of transboundary fresh waters. Recommendations are a means of expressing this regulatory power. In recognizing a basin organization's power to issue recommendations, states are at the same time giving such organizations a right to control an area that was not previously regulated.

---

130 See ICJ, Voting Procedure on Questions Relating to Reports and Petitions Concerning the Territory of South-West Africa, Advisory Opinion, 7 June 1955, at 76, where the relevant paragraph of the Advisory Opinion reads as follows: 'It is to be recalled that the Court, in its previous Opinion, stated that "The competence of the General Assembly of the United Nations to exercise such supervision and to receive and examine reports is derived from the provisions of Article 10 of the Charter, which authorizes the General Assembly to discuss any questions or any matters within the scope of the Charter and to make recommendations on these questions or matters to the Members of the United Nations." Thus, the authority of the General Assembly to exercise supervision over the administration of South-West Africa as a mandated Territory is based on the provisions of the Charter. While, in exercising that supervision, the General Assembly should not deviate from the Mandate, its authority to take decisions in order to effect such supervision is derived from its own constitution'.

1.2.2 *Methods in which Normative Powers are Exercised by Basin Organizations*

The ways in which decisions are made relate to both the rules on the attribution of normative powers and the conditions for the adoption standards. On the attribution of normative powers, in principle, a basin organization's normative competence is held by the entity, which is composed of all of its member state representatives. As with any interstate organization, the ability of basin organizations to issue standards to its members is not automatically acquired. It emanates, as a general rule, from an attribution of powers under the constituent instrument.[131] It is therefore a delegated and institutionalized normative power. As a general rule, any delegation of powers is made principally to the body which is the most representative of all member states. The idea of a community of interests and rights that underpins the cooperation of shared water resources calls for such a solution. As highlighted by the Permanent Court of International Justice in the case concerning the *Territorial Jurisdiction of the International Commission of the River Oder*, the objective is to achieve common and harmonized management that is on an equal basis and does not exclude any riparian.[132] However, the form that this institutionalization takes varies according to the profile of the basin organization.

The simplest process is provided by basin organizations with a single main plenary organ. In such cases, the commission as a plenary body exclusively enjoys standard setting powers. This is the case of the Permanent Okavango River Basin Water Commission.[133] A similar approach is also taken by the Orange-Senqu River Commission[134] and the Lake Victoria Basin Commission.[135]

In organizations where there are several principal organs standard setting powers are often attributed to the policy development and supervisory body,

131 On the legal basis of the normative activity of international organizations, see Ulfstein, *supra* note 104.

132 See PCIJ, Territorial Jurisdiction of the International Commission of the River Oder (Germany, Denmark, France, United Kingdom, Sweden and Czechoslovakia v. Poland), Judgment, 10 September 1929, at 27, para 74: 'This community of interest in a navigable river becomes the basis of a common legal right, the essential features of which are the perfect equality of all riparian States in the user of the whole course of the river and the exclusion of any preferential privilege of one riparian State in relation to the others'.

133 See OKACOM Agreement, *supra* note 47, Art. 1.

134 See Articles 3 and 5 of the Orange-Senqu River Commission Agreement, *supra* note 8, which establish that the Council is the relevant competent body that holds the standard setting powers.

135 See Articles 34 and 35 of the Lake Victoria Basin Protocol, *supra* note 11, which establish that the Sectoral Council on Lake Victoria is the relevant competent body that holds the standard setting powers.

usually the representative body at ministerial level. This is particularly the case for organizations responsible for the development of African basins. The adoption by the NBA's Council of Ministers of the Niger Basin Appendix on Environmental Protection (to the Niger Basin Water Charter) is an illustration of this.[136]

Decision-making in a basin organization's framework refers to the assessment of the conditions under which those decisions are adopted by the relevant competent body. In accordance with the scope of this study, this analysis will focus only on the adoption of decisions that are part of developing the pollution control standards process. The procedures for adopting decisions vary, depending on the institution concerned, between the methodology of voting and that of consensus.

As far as voting is concerned, practice shows a preference for the unanimity rule. The preference for this rule is certainly justified by its alleged compatibility with the sovereignty of states, as it encompasses a right of veto. Decisions adopted unanimously may be binding on states as soon as they are adopted.[137] The unanimity rule therefore preserves the freedom of action of states and in practice contributes to the spontaneous application of the decisions adopted.[138] This technique is used within the framework of the Conference of the Heads of State and the Council of Ministers of the OMVS.[139] It is worth noting that, in international practice, the scope of the unanimity rule can be attenuated in some river basin organizations. For instance, the International Commission on the Protection of the Rhine's unanimous decision-making rule (required by Article 10.1 of the Convention on the Protection of the Rhine) has the potential to be limited by the interpretation given to the legal consequences that flow from one delegation abstaining. Similar to what happens in practice with the unanimity requirement under the voting procedure of the United Nations Security Council resolutions,[140] Article 10.4 of the Convention on the

136 Niger Basin Appendix on Environmental Protection, *supra* note 103, Art. 229.

137 See M. Merle, '*Le pouvoir réglementaire des institutions internationales*', 4, Annuaire français de droit international (1958) 341–360, at 351.

138 P. Daillier, M. Forteau & A. Pellet, *Droit international public* (8th edition, Paris: LGDJ, 2009), at 693.

139 See Senegal River Organization Convention, *supra* note 31, Arts 4, 10.

140 See ICJ, Legal Consequences for States of the Continued Presence of South Africa in Namibia (South West Africa) notwithstanding Security Council Resolution 276 (1970), Advisory Opinion, 21 June 1971, at 22, para 22: 'However, the proceedings of the Security Council extending over a long period supply abundant evidence that presidential rulings and the positions taken by members of the Council, in particular its permanent members, have consistently and uniformly interpreted the practice of voluntary abstention by a permanent member as not constituting a bar to the adoption of resolutions. By abstaining, a

Protection of the Rhine provides that '[a]bstention of only one delegation shall not constitute an impediment to unanimity'. It is evident that such a provision is a way to avoid holdups due to the use of the veto from one member.

In such cases where unanimity is required, are the decisions adopted binding against the state which abstained? In some treaty regimes, abstention has the effect of limiting the application of the decision to only those states that vote for the decision.[141] The disadvantage of this *à la carte* approach is that it reduces the scope of application of these institutions and introduces a 'ratification' procedure into the normative internal decision-making process. On the basis of the rational that the institution exercises a normative power independent of that of the member states, the decisions adopted by these bodies should in principle be applicable to all member states.

Other basin organizations prefer the consensus rule to the unanimity rule. This is the case for the Assembly of the Heads of State and Government of the Volta Basin Authority,[142] the Council of Ministers of the NBA,[143] the Permanent Okavango River Basin Water Commission[144] and the Orange-Senqu River Commission.[145] The Management Committee of the Lake Tanganyika Authority also applies the consensus rule for the adoption of its decisions.[146] However, it provides for an exception to this rule with the provision of voting by way of majority in the event that consensus cannot be reached. Article 25.5 of the Lake Tanganyika Convention provides that '[i]f the Management Committee cannot reach consensus on a particular issue, it shall be re-considered at the next meeting. If consensus is still not reached, a decision may be made by a two thirds' majority of the votes of the members present and voting either in person or by proxy'.

This two thirds' majority decision-making mechanism is also provided for in the framework of the Council of Ministers of the Volta Basin Authority 'in

---

member does not signify its objection to the approval of what is being proposed; in order to prevent the adoption of a resolution requiring unanimity of the permanent members, a permanent member has only to cast a negative vote'.

141 See for example, the case of the Organisation for Economic Co-operation and Development (OECD), where Article 6.2 of the OECD Convention (1960) details the scope of abstention as follows: 'Each Member shall have one vote. If a Member abstains from voting on a decision or recommendation, such abstention shall not invalidate the decision or recommendation, which shall be applicable to the other Members but not to the abstaining Member'.

142 Volta Basin Authority Statutes, *supra* note 53, Art. 5.6.

143 Niger Basin Authority Convention, *supra* note 18, Art. 7.3.

144 OKACOM Agreement, *supra* note 47, Art. 3.5.

145 Orange-Senqu River Commission Agreement, *supra* note 8, Art. 3.9.

146 Lake Tanganyika Convention, *supra* note 9, Art. 25.5.

the event of a persistent disagreement between the State Parties'.[147] The majority mechanism, which requires a vote, is therefore not preferred within these institutions.[148] This mechanism is only used as a supplementary method to overcome a potential persistent disagreement between the parties. It is noteworthy that, in relation to the adoption of acts prescribing pollution control standards, consensus is generally favoured in basin organizations where states preserve a certain freedom in the implementation of the decisions adopted. In such cases, the application of these standards and their incorporation into domestic law is at the discretion of the state.

Part 2: The Contribution of Basin Organizations to the Implementation of Pollution Control Standards

The implementation of standards for the prevention, reduction and control of pollution constitutes the second principal area of intervention for basin organizations. In fact, the need to support riparian states in their implementation of international obligations is one of the main reasons for the establishment of these bodies. This study of the contribution of African basin organizations to the implementation of pollution control standards will therefore examine the operational arrangements that enable basin organizations to ensure the effective implementation of international standards. Although this support takes various forms, due to the variety of basin organizations, two sufficiently autonomous functions can be distinguished. The basin organization can either contribute to the implementation of standards by monitoring and controlling their implementation (I) or by providing a framework for resolving disputes that may arise between states regarding their compliance with international obligations (II).

---

147 Article 6.12 of the Volta Basin Authority Statutes, *supra* note 53, states that '[i]n the event of persistent disagreement, decisions shall be adopted by two-thirds majority of State Parties'.

148 However, the majority rule is used to take decisions relating to the general functioning of the body, including decisions on the appointment or dismissal of an international office post (see, for example, Article 12 of the Convention and Statutes relating to the development of the Chad Basin (1964), which provides that the Lake Chad Basin Commission 'shall by a simple majority, recommend to the Heads of State and Government, for the purposes of appointment, a candidate for the post of Executive Secretary' within the Lake Chad Basin Commission) or the dissolution of the body (see Article 26 of the Senegal River Organization Convention, *supra* note 31, which provides that the Conference of the Heads of State and Government may decide to dissolve the organization by a majority of the members present). See Kamto, *supra* note 19, at 905.

2.1 Monitoring and Controlling the Implementation of Pollution Control Standards

Monitoring and control activities are inherent in the functions of international organizations.[149] However, it has been observed that more than half of the treaties between countries that share transboundary rivers and lake basins do not provide for mechanisms to monitor and control their implementation.[150] This lack of monitoring and control can undermine the implementation of pollution control standards. In order to ensure compliance with their international obligations, states would therefore benefit from entrusting this monitoring and control to the relevant supervisory bodies.

Monitoring and control activities cover 'all activities by which the organisation ensures—with varying powers—that 'the organization's rules' are respected'.[151] Monitoring is more of a matter of assistance or support, whilst control is more of a technique used to compel the correction of deviant behaviour.[152] However, these two activities should be promoted and understood as being interdependent on one another due to their intrinsic and extrinsic complementarity.[153] They are in line with the approach of promoting respect for, and offering support to ensure compliance with, the law, as well as, when necessary, reacting against its violation. Through monitoring activities, basin organizations participate in the protection of transboundary water resources. We will analyse the scope of these monitoring and control activities (A) before focusing on the ways in which they are carried out (B).

149 L. Boisson de Chazournes & M. M. M. Mbengue, '*Suivi et contrôle*', in E. Lagrange and J-M. Sorel, (eds), *Traité de droit des organisations internationales* (Paris: LGDJ, 2013) 800–818, at 801. For an in-depth analysis of the monitoring and control activities of international organizations see H. Ruiz Fabri, L. A. Sicilianos & J-M. Sorel, *L'effectivité des organisations internationales: mécanismes de suivi et de contrôle* (Paris: Pedone, 2000); M. Merle, '*Le contrôle exercé par les organisations internationales sur les activités des États membres*', 5, Annuaire français de droit international (1959) 411–431; J. Charpentier, '*Le contrôle par les organisations internationales de l'exécution des obligations des États*', 4:182, Recueil des Cours, Académie de Droit International (1983), 143–246; K. Sachariew, '*Promoting Compliance with International Environmental Legal Standards: Reflections on Monitoring and Reporting Mechanisms*', 2, Yearbook of International Environmental Law (1991) 31–52.

150 United Nations Development Programme & Global Environment Facility, *Protecting International Waters—'Sustaining Livelihoods'* (New York: UNDP/GEF, 2004), at 8.

151 Boisson de Chazournes & Mbengue, *supra* note 149, at 801–802, unofficial translation of '*les activités de suivi et de contrôle englobent toutes les activités par lesquelles l'organisation s'assure—avec des pouvoirs variables—du respect des "règles de l'organisation"*'.

152 *Id*, at 804.

153 *Id*, at 809.

2.1.1 *The Scope of the Monitoring and Control Activities*

Monitoring the implementation of standards developed within the framework of basin organizations is more of a political than purely administrative exercise. On the face of it, this task seems to be carried out by the body fulfilling the function of permanent secretariat of the institution. The secretariat often has the necessary resources (staff and logistics) to fulfil this task. However, in practice, international secretariats play a simple role of transmitting or carrying out material tasks. For example, in the area of 'control', which involves correcting deviant behaviour,[154] secretariats may be empowered to collect information, by receiving or requesting it, as well as carrying out certain checks if necessary. But they do not have the capacity to exercise control themselves, and to therefore draw conclusions from the information gathered or the verifications carried out.

As a general rule, the responsibility for making findings and recommendations rests with the permanent bodies composed of state representatives. It is these bodies that receive the necessary delegation of authority to lead such processes. The logic behind this approach is to have a diplomatic, rather than contentious, approach to monitoring implementation. This is the case in the Lake Tanganyika Convention, which specifically entrusts monitoring to the Lake Tanganyika Management Committee.[155] The Management Committee is the political body of the Lake Tanganyika Authority and is composed of three members appointed by each Contracting State.[156]

The fact that the monitoring and control of the implementation of standards is entrusted to the body composed of government representatives reveals that the real purpose of these activities is not only to ensure that a state's actions comply with its international obligations, but also to enable the development of a common policy.[157] Monitoring and control therefore appear to be tools for the harmonization of basin pollution control policies.

Traditionally, the monitoring and control carried out by basin organizations has focused on the implementation of the standards set out in their constituent instruments or in the subsidiary acts adopted under such instruments. The constituent instruments of several basin organizations authorize them to ensure the application of the pollution control standards stated in their statutory texts

154 *Id*, at 804.
155 Lake Tanganyika Convention, *supra* note 9, Art. 25.7.
156 *Id*, Art. 25.1.
157 See Merle (1959), *supra* note 149, at 423.

or decisions.[158] In some cases, they enable the basin organizations to carry out general monitoring and control activities. In such circumstances, monitoring and control does not concern the application of standards for a particular sector or activity. Instead, it generally concerns the application of the relevant convention or the standards developed within the basin organization. This is usually the case for monitoring and control activities carried out under a reporting system. For instance, Article 45 of the 2003 Protocol for Sustainable Development of the Lake Victoria Basin (Lake Victoria Basin Protocol) states that '[e]ach Partner State shall periodically, at intervals to be determined by the Council, report on measures, which it has taken for the implementation of the provisions of this Protocol and their effectiveness in meeting the objectives of this Protocol'. Similarly, the Lake Tanganyika Convention requires parties to submit a regular report to the Lake Tanganyika Authority.[159]

In other cases, the monitoring and control activity is limited to a specific project or activity. This is generally the case for information procedures or the prior notification of planned activities. In such cases, the specific objective is to ensure that the actions relating to the proposed measures comply with the international standards that are in force at the basin level. The evaluation of the application for the proposed project focuses on specific elements. For example, Annex 3 to the Niger Basin Water Charter on the Prior Notification of Planned Measures in the Niger Basin requires that the Executive Secretariat of the NBA be provided with 'all the supporting technical information and data available so that the Executive Secretariat and the recipient States are able to assess the effects of the planned measures in the basin'.[160] Further, 'notification submissions must include an analysis of the cumulative impacts of the planned measures with existing projects or ongoing planned measures'.[161]

The establishment of supervisory powers to help basin organizations ensure the implementation of treaty standards (or those standards drawn up under the treaty) promotes a higher level of protection of international

158 See Danube River Convention, *supra* note 110, Art. 18; Convention on the Protection of the Rhine, *supra* note 127, Art. 8; Convention on the International Commission for the Protection of the Oder (1999), Art. 2; Great Lakes Agreement (2012) *supra* note 37, Art. 7.

159 Article 22.1 of the Lake Tanganyika Convention, *supra* note 9, states that '[e]ach Contracting State shall report periodically to the Authority on measures that it has taken to implement this Convention and on the effectiveness of these measures in meeting the objective of this Convention and on any other matters determined by a decision of the Conference of Ministers'.

160 Niger Basin Water Charter on the Prior Notification of Planned Measures and the Examination of Prior Notification Submissions (2013), Annex 3, Art. 11.

161 *Id.*

fresh-waters. However, the quality of the monitoring and control depends principally on the relevance and quality of the information that these bodies have access to. In this respect, the monitoring and control of specific activities has the advantage of preventing basin organizations from getting lost in the plethora of pollution control measures that could be adopted in order to apply the standards developed by them. Further, basin organizations are generally better equipped to judge the effectiveness of pollution control measures. In fact, a well-executed evaluation of the implementation of standards can go on to encourage the adoption of complementary measures. This highlights the preventative nature and value of monitoring and control activities in the protection of transboundary fresh waters.

2.1.2 *The Exercise of Monitoring and Control Functions*

Basin organizations have a variety of methods to monitor and control the implementation of the standards jointly adopted within them. Ongoing monitoring and control techniques (a) can be distinguished from those techniques that allow monitoring and control in specific contexts (b).

2.1.2.1 Ongoing Monitoring and Control Techniques

Ongoing monitoring and control techniques include reporting systems and technical assistance. In practice, reporting systems are a popular monitoring and control tool used by basin organizations. Generally, they are amongst the tools used to establish *a posteriori* control of state actions.[162] Reporting systems allow international commitments to be checked on a regular basis, and can help identify and suggest any necessary actions or new measures to ensure compliance with international obligations. The obligation to report to basin organizations is expressly included in several agreements on shared water resources. This is the case for the Lake Tanganyika Convention where Article 22.1 states that '[e]ach Contracting State shall report periodically to the Authority on the measures it has taken to implement this Convention and on the effectiveness of these measures in meeting the objective of this Convention and on any other matters determined by a decision of the Conference of the Ministers'.[163] A similar provision can be found in the Lake Victoria Basin Protocol.[164]

---

162 See Merle (1959), *supra* note 149, at 428–429.

163 Lake Tanganyika Convention, *supra* note 9, Art. 22.1.

164 Lake Victoria Basin Protocol, *supra* note 11, Art. 45 states: 'Each Partner State shall periodically, at intervals to be determined by the Council, report on measures, which it has taken for the implementation of the provisions of this Protocol and their effectiveness in meeting the objectives of this Protocol'.

These reports generally must meet requirements of form and substance. In terms of form, it is particularly worth noting the frequency of reporting. Treaty practice is generally silent on this point.[165] States are simply invited to submit their reports to the basin organization on a 'regular' basis. In any event, with respect to pollution control standards, the frequency of reporting must be determined by taking into account the minimum time required for states to adopt domestic measures in accordance with international standards. The frequency of reporting also depends on the time required to assess the impact of water quality measures.

As for the substantive requirements, it should be noted that the content of these reports is not left to the discretion of states. Practice tends to indicate that a minimum level of information should be provided. Accordingly, Article 22.1 of the Lake Tanganyika Convention provides that reports shall include, in particular,

(a) information on the laws and administrative procedures of the Contracting State regulating, or relevant to the prevention, control and reduction of adverse impacts;
(b) legal, administrative and other measures taken relating to the assessment of the environmental impact of proposed activities and measures ...;
(c) information on the state of the Lake Basin within the territory of the Contracting State; and
(d) measures taken to implement the provisions of this Convention or to further the attainment of its objective.

Further, due to this reporting obligation, basin organizations can assess any follow-up action that parties take further to their recommendations. The right to evaluate in this way may lead to the formulation of new recommendations in the event of shortcomings in the implementation of their earlier recommendations or the discovery of new problem areas.

If we evaluate this reporting system against the rationale of anticipating the impacts of pollution, its weakness is essentially due to the *ex post* assessment of the state's implementation of certain international standards (such as those which set a maximum permitted level of pollutants). It follows that

165 An exception is provided by the practice of the International Joint Commission between Canada and the United States of America which requires that a report is submitted by each party every three years. Under Article 5.2(e) of the Great Lakes Agreement (2012), *supra* note 37, the parties provide their progress reports prior to every Great Lakes Public Forum 'to document actions relating to this Agreement'. As provided in Article 5.1, these forums are held every three years to discuss progress and receive public comments and input on the state of the lakes and the progress report of the parties. For further information, see the IJC website: http://www.ijc.org, accessed 23 January 2020.

the effectiveness of any measures adopted by states to comply with international standards can only be assessed once any damage due to pollution has occurred.

The presence of technical assistance can often address this weakness in the reporting system. In practice, it is often teamed up with a reporting system. Technical assistance is a mechanism whereby a basin organization provides assistance in a specific area to a requesting state. As such, it is a mechanism for providing services to states party to a basin organization.[166] Technical assistance is also an excellent tool for monitoring the implementation of standards jointly adopted by states within the organization. Indeed, through this assistance, the institution can encourage and support states to adopt measures in accordance with those international standards in force. Technical assistance has a preventative nature due to its ability to anticipate non-compliance with such standards.

In general, technical assistance is not expressly mentioned amongst the responsibilities of basin organizations. It can be exercised, however, through a basin organization's general function to provide advice to parties on issues that may arise in the management and protection of water resources. For example, Article 4 of the 1994 Agreement on the Establishment of a Permanent Okavango River Basin Water Commission assigns to the Commission the function 'to advise the Contracting Parties on … the prevention of the pollution of water resources and the control over aquatic weeds in the Okavango River Basin'. A similar advisory function is planned for the Orange-Senqu River Commission[167] and the Limpopo River Commission.[168]

2.1.2.2 Monitoring and Control Techniques in Specific Contexts

The common feature of monitoring and control techniques used for specific circumstances is that they are based on the principle that no activity or action of a certain magnitude can take place without prior notification being given to the basin organization. In such a way, the basin organization has a form of *a priori* control over the actions of any state planning such an activity. The basin organization can therefore verify, through the information provided by the state concerned, whether the project takes into account current international

166 G. Cahin, '*La variété des fonctions imparties aux organisations internationales*', in E. Lagrange & J.-M. Sorel, (eds), *Traité de droit des organisations internationales* (Paris: LGDJ, 2013) 671–704, at 698–699.

167 Orange-Senqu River Commission Agreement, *supra* note 8, Art. 5.

168 Limpopo Watercourse Commission Agreement, *supra* note 10, Art. 7.

standards and, if necessary, propose measures to ensure compliance with such standards.

Prior agreement is the strictest procedure. It is provided for in the Convention on the Status of Senegal River in these terms: 'No project likely to significantly alter the characteristics of the river system, its navigability, agricultural or industrial conditions, the health of the waters, the biological characteristics of its fauna or flora, its water body, may be carried out without prior approval by the Contracting States after discussion and justification of any objections'.[169] The Senegal River Water Charter provides further clarification by providing that this prior approval is the exclusive responsibility of the OMVS Council of Ministers, after having consulted with the Permanent Water Commission.[170]

Other institutions use more flexible courses of action. For example, an assent and prior information procedure forms the practice of the Lake Chad Basin Commission. Article 24 of the Lake Chad Basin Water Charter requires prior authorization for the discharge of pollutants that may pose a risk to public health and safety or cause harmful effects to the Lake Chad Basin's biodiversity. Further, Article 25.1 of the Lake Chad Basin Water Charter states that '[a]uthorizations to discharge shall be issued by the State Parties to any public or private individual person or entity having duly applied for such authorization in accordance with national procedure'.[171]

However, Article 25.2 of the Lake Chad Basin Water Charter requires that 'State Parties shall submit all applications for authorization to discharge made to them to the Commission to obtain its opinion'.[172] Through this procedure, the Lake Chad Basin Commission can assess whether the application for authorization to discharge complies with current international standards. The Commission's assessment criteria include 'the nature of the pollutants and the fragility and hydrological and ecological characteristics of the receiving environment'.[173] To this end, the Commission maintains a database on pollutant discharges and may use its hydrological model of the Lake Chad Basin and its knowledge of the aquatic environment to assess the appropriateness of any application submitted to it requesting authorization to discharge pollutants.[174]

The Lake Chad Basin Commission's assent procedure is also relevant in that it constitutes a form of monitoring and control of the activity of non-state actors.

169 Convention on the Status of the Senegal River (1972), Art. 4.1 [Status of the Senegal River Convention]; see also Senegal River Water Charter, *supra* note 84, Art. 10.

170 Senegal River Water Charter, *id*, Art. 11.

171 Lake Chad Basin Water Charter, *supra* note 100, Art. 25.1.

172 *Id*, Art. 25.2.

173 *Id*, Art. 25.3.

174 *Id*.

Prior authorization is in principle granted after monitoring the measures taken by any project to discharge pollutants in order to reduce the risk of damage to water quality. However, as the discharge of pollutants can also be carried out by private individuals and legal entities, the prior authorization requirement leads to the control of measures adopted by such non-state actors. The assent procedure therefore allows the Lake Chad Basin Commission to verify whether these actors have, for example, respected the current water quality standards or implemented the best techniques or environmental practices.

Nevertheless, this power of control granted to the Lake Chad Basin Commission through the assent procedure is mitigated by the provision of a time limit. The Lake Chad Basin Commission has only three months to provide an opinion on all applications for authorization to discharge.[175] During this period, the state party is required to refrain from authorizing the activity.[176] However, the Lake Chad Basin Water Charter does not specify the legal consequences if the Commission gives an unfavourable opinion after the three month period. It merely states that the state party may 'proceed to respond to the applicant without the opinion of the Commission' after the deadline has passed.[177] This legal uncertainty reduces the effectiveness of the mechanism. To give full effect to the assent procedure, the most viable option would be to give the Lake Chad Basin Commission the ability to make recommendations in the event of an unfavourable opinion (issued after the three month period) in order to reduce the risk of significant damage to the resource. The state party that submitted the request for authorization would then be tasked with ensuring that these recommendations were taken into account in the project to discharge pollutants before granting its final authorization.

An example of the prior information procedure is provided for in paragraph 1 of Article 7 of the 1975 Statute of the River Uruguay, which requires the state of origin of any proposed activity on the Uruguay River to notify CARU so that it can determine 'on a preliminary basis and within a maximum period of 30 days whether the plan might cause significant damage to the other Party'.[178] Unlike the prior agreement procedure, this procedure does not aim to lead to an authorization by the Commission for the implementation of the project, but rather to assess whether the project falls within the scope of activities requiring the fulfilment of procedural obligations of cooperation, in this case those of notification and consultation between the parties. Therefore it favours

175 *Id*, Art. 25.2.

176 *Id.*

177 *Id.*

178 Statute of the River Uruguay (1975), Art. 7.1.

the monitoring and control of the proper performance of the obligation not to cause significant damage. The ICJ highlighted this in the case concerning *Pulp Mills on the River Uruguay*. As a reminder, this case involved the states of Argentina and Uruguay in relation to the construction of two pulp mills (the 'Celulosa de M'Bopicuá S. A.' mill and the 'Orion' mill) on the left bank of the Uruguay River, opposite the Argentine region of Gualeguaychú. Among Argentina's main claims against Uruguay was its violation of the obligation under paragraph 1 of Article 7 of the Statute of the River Uruguay. This article requires prior notice to be given by state parties to CARU for all 'works which are liable to affect navigation, the régime of the river or the quality of its waters'.[179]

The Court noted that, whilst the parties agreed that CARU should be notified of the two pulp mill projects and the plan to build the port terminal at Fray Bentos, they were nevertheless opposed in relation to the content of the information required to be provided to CARU and the timing of its transmission.[180] For Argentina, the obligation to provide information had to be determined in light of the objective of preventing damage to navigation, the river régime or water quality.[181] In other words, in the present case, in Argentina's view, CARU must be informed of the plan prior to the authorization and construction of a project on the Uruguay River.[182] Uruguay, on the other hand, considered that the information did not have to be provided to CARU in the early stages of planning. Uruguay's argument was that CARU would not have sufficient information at this early stage to determine whether or not the plans were likely to cause significant damage to the other state.[183] In order to make this assessment, Uruguay considered that the project would need to reach a stage where the state would have all the necessary technical information at its disposal.

The Court did not accept Uruguay's argument. After recalling the customary nature of the principle of prevention,[184] the Court stressed that the obligation to inform CARU 'allows for the initiation of co-operation between the Parties

179 *Id.*

180 See Pulp Mills Judgment, *supra* note 2, at 55, para 98.

181 *Id*, para 99.

182 *Id.*

183 *Id*, para 100.

184 *Id*, para 101 where the Court pointed out that 'the principle of prevention, as a customary rule, has its origin in the due diligence of a State on its territory. It is "every State's obligation not to allow knowingly its territory to be used for acts contrary to the rights of other States" (*Corfu Channel (United Kingdom v. Albania), Merits, Judgment, I. C. J. Reports 1949*, p. 22). A State is thus required to use all means at its disposal in order to avoid activities which take place on its territory, or in any area under its jurisdiction, causing significant damage to the environment of another State'.

which is necessary in order to fulfil the obligation of prevention'.[185] In light of this preventative purpose, the Court held:

> The Court considers that the State planning activities referred to in Article 7 of the Statute is required to inform CARU as soon as it is in possession of a plan which is sufficiently developed to enable CARU to make the preliminary assessment (required by paragraph 1 of that provision) of whether the proposed works might cause significant damage to the other party. At that stage, the information provided will not necessarily consist of a full assessment of the environmental impact of the project, which will often require further time and resources, although, where more complete information is available, this should, of course, be transmitted to CARU to give it the best possible basis on which to make its preliminary assessment. In any event, the duty to inform CARU will become applicable at the stage when the relevant authority has had the project referred to it with the aim of obtaining initial environmental authorization and before the granting of that authorization.[186]

The various mechanisms examined above highlight the contribution of monitoring and control functions to help ensure states' compliance with the international obligations. By supervising their implementation and reacting to situations of state non-compliance with the rules adopted under a basin organization's framework, these monitoring and control mechanisms are also intended to help prevent the tensions (that may surround an activity that is likely to cause pollution damage) from escalating to the dispute stage. In this respect, monitoring and control activities are effective governance tools for the prevention of disputes.

2.2 Basin Organizations and Dispute Settlement

The obligation to settle disputes peacefully is an obligation under general international law, and is also contained in the Charter of the United Nations.[187]

185 *Id*, para 102.

186 *Id*, para 105.

187 United Nations Charter (1945), Arts 1.1, 2.3. On international dispute settlement in International Law, see L. Boisson de Chazournes, M. Kohen & J. E. Viñuales, (eds), *Diplomatic and Judicial Means of Dispute Settlement* (Leiden: Martinus Nijhoff, 2013); J. G. Merrills, *International Dispute Settlement* (Cambridge: Cambridge University Press, 2011) ; J. Collier & A. V. Lowe, *The Settlement of Disputes in International Law* (Oxford: Oxford University

It therefore equally applies to disputes that arise in connection with the pollution of international fresh waters. African basin organizations have played a crucial role in this field of dispute settlement.[188] Whilst practice shows a strong emphasis on the 'outsourcing' of dispute settlement by basins organizations (A), such institutions may nevertheless intervene directly by providing a framework for the dispute resolution procedure. This intervention reflects the growing trend of 'in-house' dispute resolution within basin organizations (B).

2.2.1 *The Outsourcing of Dispute Settlement Procedures*

The 'outsourcing' (or 'externalization') of dispute settlement procedures refers to the phenomenon of international freshwater pollution dispute resolution taking place outside of the basin organization. This is often the result of the content of the constituent instruments of these institutions. The dispute resolution mechanisms available to members of the organization range from diplomatic (a) to judicial means (b). The diplomatic dispute settlement methods are the final options for parties before the matter is referred to a judicial body.

2.2.1.1 Diplomatic Means of Dispute Settlement

In terms of diplomatic means of dispute resolution, water agreements provide for either direct negotiations between the parties or the intervention of a third party. When a water dispute arises, negotiation is generally considered to be the minimum level of dispute resolution.[189] Negotiations often precede the use of alternative dispute resolution mechanisms.[190] It is generally the failure of negotiations that triggers the use of other dispute settlement methods. The

---

Press, 1999); United Nations, *Handbook on the Peaceful Settlement of International Disputes between States* (New York: United Nations, 1992); On dispute settlement in water disputes, see in particular S. C. McCaffrey, *The Law of International Watercourses* (Oxford: Oxford University Press, 2019), at 570–580; L. Boisson de Chazournes, *Fresh Water in International Law* (Oxford: Oxford University Press, 2013), at 197–249.

188 On the contribution of basin organizations to the resolution of disputes in international freshwater management, see in particular McCaffrey, *supra* note 187, at 575–578; Boisson de Chazournes (2013), *id*, at 181–184; E. Brown Weiss, *International Law in a Water-Scarce World* (Leiden/Boston: Brill, 2013), at 179–180; L. Boisson de Chazournes & M. Tignino, '*Le règlement des différends internationaux relatifs à l'eau*', in Conseil d'Etat (ed.), *L'eau et son droit. Etudes et documents du Conseil d'État* (Paris: La documentation française, 2010) 489–514.

189 See Brown Weiss, *id*, at 179–180; I. Dombrowsky, *Conflict, Cooperation, and Institutions in International Water Management: An Economic Analysis* (Cheltenham: Edward Elgar, 2007), at 142; Boisson de Chazournes & Tignino, *id*, at 491.

190 Boisson de Chazournes & Tignino, *id*, at 491.

2002 Tripartite Interim Agreement for Co-operation on the Protection and Sustainable Utilisation of the Water Resources of the Incomati and Maputo Watercourses (Incomati and Maputo Watercourses Agreement) ensures this order of priority by setting a specific time period for the completion of negotiations. Thus, Article 15 of the Incomati and Maputo Watercourses Agreement provides:

(1) Any dispute between the Parties concerning the interpretation or implementation of this Agreement shall be settled amicably through consultation and negotiations between the Parties.

(2) Where the dispute has not been settled within one year, from the date upon which such negotiations were requested, it may be submitted to arbitration by either Party.

Direct negotiations allow parties to identify the different interests at stake and reach compromises that are favourable to all. Negotiations take place through official channels, hence their diplomatic nature. The most common form is negotiation through embassies or between senior officials of foreign ministries, foreign ministers, or at the very top of the state apparatus, the heads of state. However, negotiations at a very political level may include technical aspects. This form of negotiation appears to be more suitable for disputes with strong technical connotations, such as those relating to pollution.

Although these are negotiations envisaged outside of the basin organizations, basin organizations may be permitted to intervene in the process. This does not in itself lead to the 'internalization' of the settlement of the dispute, as this degree of involvement is not intended to entrust the organization with the task of leading the process, but to assist states in the negotiation process. Generally, assistance is limited to the management of information relating to the dispute during the negotiation. The Lake Tanganyika Convention thus requires the Contracting States concerned to notify the Secretariat of the Lake Tanganyika Authority of any disputes that arise between them.[191] The Secretariat is then responsible for informing the other Contracting States of the existence and nature of the dispute.[192] Similar communications may be relevant in cases where the basin is shared by more than two states. Once

191 Lake Tanganyika Convention, *supra* note 9, Art. 29.1. See also in the same sense, Danube River Convention, *supra* note 110, Art. 24.2(a): 'If the parties to the dispute are unable to settle the dispute in accordance with paragraph 1 of this Article within a reasonable time, but not more than twelve months after the International Commission has been notified about the dispute by a party to the dispute, the dispute shall be submitted for compulsory decision to one of the following means of peaceful settlement'.

192 Lake Tanganyika Convention, *supra* note 9, Art. 29.1.

informed, third party riparian states to the dispute may volunteer to help facilitate negotiations between the parties.

In terms of the actual conduct of the negotiation process, in accordance with the principle of good faith, '[the parties] are under an obligation so to conduct themselves that the negotiations are meaningful'.[193] As recalled by the Lake Chad Basin Water Charter, negotiations must be conducted 'in good faith with a desire to come to an agreement'.[194] However, this obligation to negotiate does not amount to an obligation to reach an agreement.[195]

The failure of negotiations generally leads to the use of third parties. The use of third parties other than basin organizations is evident in several international instruments adopted under basin organization frameworks. Parties to a dispute generally have a choice between informal and formal means of dispute resolution. Mediation and good offices are the informal means of dispute resolution *par excellence*.[196] These types of intervention have been provided for in several basin agreements.[197] It is important to make the distinction between mediation and good offices. Whilst good offices are more discreet, mediation plays a more active role.[198] Indeed, a mediator is involved in the negotiations between the parties to the dispute and offers the parties a solution to their disagreement. However, the solution proposed by the mediator is not binding, unless the parties so agree.[199] For good offices, the third party merely encourages the parties to settle their disputes amicably.[200] To this end, it promotes meetings between the parties and facilitates communication between them in order to help them work together to resolve their disagreement.

Water agreements also provide for more formal diplomatic channels in order to settle disputes, such as fact-finding investigations or conciliation[201]

193 ICJ, North Sea Continental Shelf, Judgment, 20 February 1969, at 47, para 85; Pulp Mills Judgment, *supra* note 2, at 67, para 146.

194 Lake Chad Basin Water Charter, *supra* note 100, Art. 86.2.

195 PCIJ, Rail Traffic between Lithuania and Poland, Advisory Opinion, 15 October 1931, Series A/B No. 42, at 116; Pulp Mills Judgment, *supra* note 2, at 68, para 150.

196 See Brown Weiss, *supra* note 188, at 139.

197 See, for example, Agreement on the Nile River Basin Cooperative Framework (2010), Art. 34; Lake Tanganyika Convention, *supra* note 9, Arts 29.2(1); Lake Chad Basin Water Charter, *supra* note 100, Art. 88; Senegal River Organization Convention, *supra* note 31, Art. 24; Status of the Senegal River Convention, *supra* note 169, Art. 18.

198 *Id.*

199 *Id.*

200 See Brown Weiss, *supra* note 188, at 139.

201 Lake Tanganyika Convention, *supra* note 9, Art. 29.2(b); Framework Agreement on the Sava River Basin (2002), Art. 22.2 [Sava River Basin Framework Agreement]; Senegal River Water Charter, *supra* note 84, Art. 30; Senegal River Organization Convention, *supra* note 31, Art. 24; Status of the Senegal River Convention, *supra* note 169, Art. 18.

carried out by commissions composed of persons trusted by the parties.[202] In this respect, they constitute institutionalized means of settling disputes. Whilst the purpose of an investigation is in principle to establish facts, the purpose of conciliation is much broader: to direct the parties towards a solution, without, however, being automatically binding.[203] In both cases, the procedures require the consent and cooperation of the parties to the dispute for their implementation.[204]

With respect to the choice of the third parties involved, whilst some instruments remain silent on the method of appointment, other agreements are more specific. For instance, the Lake Tanganyika Convention specifies the following with regard to the mediation procedure: 'If the States concerned cannot settle the dispute through negotiation they shall agree in good faith a dispute settlement procedure, which may include ... jointly seeking the ... mediation by a third party (which shall be a Contracting State that is not involved in the dispute)'.[205]

The mediation procedure is therefore limited in scope to the basin states party to the Lake Tanganyika Convention. In contrast, the Lake Tanganyika Convention excludes the appointment of Contracting State nationals as members of the fact-finding commission: 'The Executive Director of the Secretariat shall convene a fact-finding Commission composed of one person nominated by each Party. None of these persons shall be a national of one of the Contracting States'.[206] Further, 'If one of the parties fails to nominate a member within three months of the initial request ... any other Party may request the Secretary-General of the African Union to appoint a person who does not have the nationality of any of the Contracting States, as a single member Commission'.[207]

This dual approach to the selection of the third party is probably due to the nature of the different dispute resolution processes. Whilst mediation involves a certain proximity between the potential mediator and the state parties to the dispute, an inquiry by its very purpose requires greater independence and impartiality of the commissioners. The principal concern in an inquiry is to use experts qualified in the field where the dispute arose and who will not be influenced by government authorities in their work.

---

202 P.-M. Dupuy & Y. Kerbrat, *Droit international public* (Paris: Dalloz, 2018), at 618.

203 *Id.*

204 *Id.*

205 Lake Tanganyika Convention , *supra* note 9, Art. 29.2(a).

206 *Id*, Annex III, Art. 2.1.

207 *Id*, Annex III, Art. 2.4.

Other agreements indicate a preference for broader regionalization in the selection of third parties in both formal and informal dispute resolution processes. The Lake Chad Basin Water Charter, for example, allows one of the state parties to the dispute to 'bring the case before the competent regional and sub-regional authorities, which shall in turn undertake the conduct of good offices or mediation procedures' in the event that the Lake Chad Basin Commission is unable to settle the dispute.[208] Other African agreements explicitly refer to the dispute settlement functions of the Organization of African Unity. This is the case with the OMVS fundamental texts[209] and the 1977 Agreement for the establishment of the Organization for the Management and Development of the Kagera River Basin.[210] The Charter of the Organization of African Unity provides for the 'peaceful settlement of disputes by negotiation, mediation, conciliation or arbitration'[211] and established for this purpose a Commission for Mediation, Conciliation and Arbitration by means of a separate protocol.[212] This 21-member Commission can be seized by the parties to a dispute to conduct mediation[213] or conciliation.[214] Although the Mediation Commission was not maintained following the replacement of the Organization of African Unity by the African Union,[215] the African Union can still be requested to mediate or

208 Lake Chad Basin Water Charter, *supra* note 100, Art. 88.

209 See Article 24 of the Senegal River Organization Convention, *supra* note 31, which states: 'Any dispute that may arise between the Contracting States concerning the interpretation or application of this Convention shall be resolved through conciliation and mediation. Failing agreement, the Contracting States shall refer the matter to the Conciliation and Arbitration Commission of the Organization of African Unity'. A similar provision is found in Article 18 of the Status of the Senegal River Convention *supra* note 169, and Article 30 of the Senegal River Water Charter, *supra* note 84 (with the Charter making reference to the Organization of African Unity).

210 See Article 18 of the Agreement for the Establishment of the Organization for the Management and Development of the Kagera River Basin (1977): 'In the event of a dispute arising out of the application of this Agreement, that dispute shall be resolved by consultation among the States involved or in the case of failure the Parties to the dispute will resort to the procedures as laid down in the Charter of the Organization of African Unity'.

211 Charter of the Organization of African Unity (1963), Art. III.4.

212 *Id*, Art. XIX. With respect to the Commission, see T. O. Elias, '*The Commission of Mediation, Conciliation and Arbitration of the Organization of African Unity*', 41, British Yearbook of International Law (1964) 336–354.

213 Protocol Relating to the Commission of Mediation, Conciliation and Arbitration of the Organization of African Unity (1964), Part Three.

214 *Id*, Part Four.

215 Some authors have also stressed the need to review the dispute settlement procedures provided for in any agreements implicated in light of these new developments. See in particular, A. Samboly Ba & M. M. Mbengue, '*Le régime juridique du fleuve Sénégal: Aspect*

provide good offices between state parties to a dispute. It is also able to act on its own initiative if the dispute in question threatens international peace and security.[216]

That being said, it could also be relevant for African basin legal frameworks to anticipate options that allow universalization in the selection of third parties. Indeed, the majority of instruments seem to limit access to the good offices of global organizations such as the World Bank or the United Nations. However, the contribution of these global organizations can be useful or even decisive in facilitating the settlement of disputes and therefore their involvement needs to be more explicit. In this context, it may be recalled that in November 2012 a mechanism to support implementation and compliance, the Implementation Committee, was established by Decision VI/1 of the Meeting of the Parties of the Water Convention.[217] The objective of the mechanism is to 'facilitate, promote and safeguard the implementation and application of and compliance with the Convention'.[218] The Implementation Committee's functions can be triggered through an advisory procedure whereby parties may request advice, submissions by parties (either by a party experiencing problems with its implementation of, or compliance with the Convention, or by a party affected by another party's difficulty in implementation and compliance), and action by the Committee on its own initiative. The Implementation Committee consists of nine members, who serve in their personal capacity

---

du droit des cours d'eau dans un contexte régional', 12, African Yearbook of International Law (2006) 309–347, at 322.

216 A Peace and Security Council was established under the Protocol relating to the Establishment of the Peace and Security Council of the African Union (2002) to the Constitutive Act of the African Union. Under Article 8.5 of the 2002 Protocol, the Peace and Security Council may decide to establish 'ad hoc committees for mediation, conciliation or enquiry' consisting of one or more states parties to facilitate the settlement of disputes and prevention of conflicts if there is a risk of events escalating towards an armed conflict.

217 UNECE, *Report of the Meeting of the Parties on its Sixth Session. Addendum. Decisions and Vision for the Future of the Convention*, UNECE Doc. ECE/MP.WAT/37/Add.2 (2012), at 2; on the Water Convention Implementation Committee see J. G. Lammers, '*The Interplay between the UN Watercourses Convention and the UNECE Convention on the Protection and Use of Transboundary Watercourses and International Lakes*', in L. Boisson de Chazournes et al (eds.), *The UN Convention on the Law of the Non- Navigational Uses of International Watercourse: A Commentary* (Oxford: Oxford University Press, 2018) 423–424; A. Tanzi & C. Contartese, '*Dispute Prevention, Dispute Settlement and Implementation Facilitation in International Water Law: The Added Value of the Establishment of an Implementation Mechanism Under the Water Convention*', in A. Tanzi et al (eds), *The UNECE Convention on the Protection and Use of Transboundary Watercourses and International Lakes* (Leiden/Boston: Brill/Nijhoff, 2015) 317–329.

218 UNECE, *id*, at 2.

and aims to be 'simple, non-confrontational, non-adversarial, transparent, supportive and cooperative in nature'.[219] Therefore, it may serve as a means to prevent situations escalating into a dispute. The trend towards accession to the Water Convention by African countries should also be teamed whenever possible with the consideration of the good offices of the Implementation Committee as a potential dispute settlement option.

2.2.1.2 Judicial Means of Dispute Settlement

Referral to international courts is the ultimate method of dispute resolution generally offered to member states of basin organizations under their legal instruments. Such judicial means of dispute settlement can range from establishing arbitral tribunals to resorting to permanent courts.

Arbitration is by far the oldest and most frequent form of judicial settlement in water matters.[220] It is therefore quite normal that it can be found in the legal instruments of several basin organizations. In Africa, apart from the OMVS,[221] arbitration is one of the judicial dispute resolution mechanisms provided for in several agreements, including the Lake Chad Basin Water Charter,[222] and it is the final means of dispute resolution in the Incomati and Maputo Watercourses Agreement[223] and the Lake Tanganyika Convention.[224]

Ultimately, the use of arbitration remains the preferred method of settling disputes over transboundary water resources. Some instruments also provide the detail of any such arbitral proceedings in an appendix, including relevant time limits and the composition of the arbitral tribunal.[225] This practice is in

---

219 *Id.*

220 See Boisson de Chazournes & Tignino, *supra* note 188. With respect to the use of arbitration in water disputes see also Brown Weiss, *supra* note 188, at 133–135.

221 See Senegal River Water Charter, *supra* note 84, Art. 30; Senegal River Organization Convention, *supra* note 31, Art. 24; Status of the Senegal River Convention, *supra* note 169, Art. 18. These provisions refer in particular to the Mediation, Conciliation and Arbitration Commission of the Organization of the African Unity/Union. As noted, these provisions need updating due to the fact that the said Commission no longer exists.

222 Lake Chad Basin Water Charter, *supra* note 100, Art. 89.

223 Tripartite Interim Agreement between the Republic of Mozambique and the Republic of South Africa and the Kingdom of Swaziland for Co-operation on the Protection and Sustainable Utilisation of the Water Resources of the Incomati and Maputo Watercourses (2002), Art. 15.

224 Lake Tanganyika Convention, *supra* note 9, Art. 29.2(c).

225 See for example, the following annexes on arbitration procedure: Lake Tanganyika Convention, *supra* note 9, Annex IV; Sava River Basin Framework Agreement, *supra* note 201, Annex II; Convention on the Protection of the Rhine, *supra* note 127, Annex; Danube River Convention, *supra* note 110, Annex V; Convention on the Protection of the Rhine against Pollution by Chlorides (1976), Annex B.

line with the Water Convention and the Watercourses Convention, both of which contain an annex with detailed provisions relating to arbitration. With the opening of the Water Convention to universal accession[226] and the entry into force of the Watercourses Convention,[227] it is expected that arbitration will be promoted in the agreements adopted within the framework of basin organizations as a method of dispute settlement.

Provisions that provide recourse to permanent courts are common in the constituent treaties that establish basin organizations and in the agreements adopted under their frameworks. In such instances, provision for recourse to the ICJ prevails. The OMVS Conventions consider the ICJ as the last resort following the failure of diplomatic and judicial dispute settlement procedures.[228] The Niger Basin Water Charter[229] and the Lake Chad Basin Water Charter follow an identical approach.[230]

Nevertheless, in African practice there is a trend towards the regionalization of judicial settlement of disputes. Indeed, several treaties that establish Southern African basin organizations provide for the referral to the Southern African Development Community Tribunal established under the 1992 Treaty of the Southern African Development Community as a last resort.[231] For example, such a referral is promoted by the SADC Revised Protocol, which serves

226 In November 2003, an amendment was made to Articles 25 and 26 in order to open the Water Convention (1992) to universal accession. These amendments entered into force on 6 February 2013. Through these amendments, United Nations member states that are outside of the UNECE region can become parties to the Water Convention. See UNECE, *Introduction: About the UNECE Water Convention*, http://www.unece.org/env/water/text/text.html (accessed 23 January, 2020); see also I. Trombitcaia & S. Koeppel, *'From a Regional towards a Global Instrument: The 2003 Amendment to the UNECE Water Convention'*, in A. Tanzi et al (eds), *The UNECE Convention on the Protection and Use of Transboundary Watercourses and International Lakes* (Leiden/Boston: Brill/Nijhoff, 2015) 15–31.

227 The Watercourses Convention on the Law of the Non-navigational Use of Watercourses 1997 [Watercourses Convention] entered into force on 17 August 2014.

228 See Senegal River Water Charter, *supra* note 84, Art. 30; Senegal River Organization Convention, *supra* note 31, Art. 24; Status of the Senegal River Convention, *supra* note 169, Art. 18.

229 See Niger Basin Water Charter, *supra* note 97, Art. 31.

230 See Lake Chad Basin Water Charter, *supra* note 100, Art. 89.

231 Examples of provisions in treaties where reference is made to the Southern African Development Community Tribunal include the Zambezi River Commission Agreement (2004), Art. 21.3, the Limpopo River Commission Agreement, *supra* note 18, Art. 9.2, and the Orange-Senqu River Commission Agreement, *supra* note 8, Art. 8.2.

as a model instrument in the region.[232] Similarly, the Volta Basin Authority Convention requires member states, in the event of the failure of diplomatic dispute settlement methods, to 'submit the matter to one of the competent organs of ECOWAS [the Economic Community of West African States] or [the] African Union' and before any submission to the ICJ.[233] However, in addition to diplomatic settlement procedures, these two organizations offer judicial mechanisms, including the Court of Justice of ECOWAS and the African Union Court of Justice. In the absence of details on these particular mechanisms and how they interrelate, the option for member states to use the judicial mechanisms made available by regional organizations for the settlement of their disputes remains open. Consequently, the primacy thus accorded to the referral to these regional bodies by the convention before any referral to the ICJ regionalizes judicial settlements. This is part of a classic approach to dispute resolution in African waterways as explained by Mutoy Mubiala in the following terms: 'In this field, the search for an African solution is the priority, with judicial settlement institutions outside of the continent being mentioned or used in a very marginal way. This results from the influence of the legal framework of the OAU [Organization of African Unity] on the functioning of African regional or sub-regional organizations'.[234]

However, some authors have expressed doubts over the ability of African judicial institutions to resolve water-related disputes. Their main argument was that the scope of these institutions' jurisdiction was limited to disputes arising from the interpretation and application of their constituent treaties.[235] In practice, the subject does not pose much difficulty. For instance, the Southern African Development Community Tribunal's jurisdiction is derived from both the combined and intersecting provisions of the Treaty of the Southern African

232 Article 7.2 of the SADC Shared Watercourses Protocol (2000) states that '[d]isputes between State Parties regarding the interpretation or application of the provisions of this Protocol which are not settled amicably, shall be referred to the Tribunal'.

233 Volta River Basin Authority Convention, *supra* note 16, Art. 13.3.

234 M. Mubiala, '*Le régionalisme africain en droit international fluvial*', 6 African Journal of International and Comparative Law (1994) 449–471, at 470, unofficial translation: '*dans ce domaine, la recherche d'une solution africaine se fait à titre principal, les institutions de règlement extérieures au continent étant mentionnées ou mises à contribution de façon tout à fait marginale. C'est le résultat de l'influence du système juridique de l'OUA* [*l'Organisation de l'unité africaine*] *sur le fonctionnement des organisations africaines à vocation régionale ou sous-régionale*'.

235 See Garané, *supra* note 46, at 137.

Development Community[236] and the legal instruments of the basin organizations. Similarly, with respect to the jurisdiction of the ECOWAS Court of Justice, Article 3.6 of the 2005 Supplementary Protocol amending Articles relating to the Community Court of Justice extends the Court's jurisdiction: 'The Court shall have jurisdiction over any matter provided for in an agreement where the parties provide that the Court shall settle disputes arising from the agreement'.

Finally, it is difficult to argue that Article 19.1(c) of the Protocol of the Court of Justice of the African Union, which extends the Court's jurisdiction to 'any question of international law', is limited to matters that only clearly relate to the Constitutive Act of the African Union, particularly in view of its expanded mandate, of which the Court of Justice is a permanent body. In addition, there is no practice to support such a limitation.[237]

On the other hand, the relationship that some international instruments establish between regional dispute settlement mechanisms and the ICJ raises some questions. For example, Article 13.3 of the Volta Basin Authority Convention stipulates that '[i]n the absence of an amicable settlement, the Parties shall submit the matter to one of the competent organs of ECOWAS or the African Union and thereafter to the International Court of Justice'. By using the term 'thereafter', this provision puts in place a *prima facie* 'order of priority of referral' between the various judicial mechanisms. Article 13.3 could be criticized for establishing a questionable form of judicial hierarchy comprising of 'first instance' regional courts and a 'last instance' ICJ.[238] In addition, there is a risk that this provision could raise a jurisdictional conflict issue. In fact, judgments delivered by these regional courts are generally final[239] and can only be reviewed by the court that delivered them.[240] The question then focuses on whether the ICJ has jurisdiction to hear a dispute a regional court

---

236 Article 16.1 of the Treaty of the Southern African Development Community (1992) states: 'The Tribunal shall be constituted to ensure adherence to and the proper interpretation of the provisions of this Treaty and subsidiary instruments and to adjudicate upon such disputes as may be referred to it'.

237 In favour of the thesis of restricting questions to the constituent treaty, see in particular, Garané, *supra* note 46, at 137.

238 See Article 13.3 of the Volta River Basin Authority Convention, *supra* note 16: 'In the absence of amicable settlement, the Parties shall submit the matter to one of the competent organs of ECOWAS or the African Union and thereafter to the International Court of Justice'.

239 See Protocol of the Court of Justice of the African Union (2003), Art. 35; Protocol on the Community [ECOWAS] Court of Justice (1991), Art. 19.

240 See Article 40 of the Protocol of the Court of Justice of the African Union, *id*: 'In the event of any dispute as to the meaning or scope of the judgment, the Court shall construe it upon the request of any of the parties'.

has already decided upon. An examination of the relevant provisions which relate to the jurisdiction of regional courts suggests a *priori* that the response to this question is a negative one. However, it is important to put this into perspective. Indeed, by allowing parties to submit proceedings to the ICJ as a 'last resort', Article 13.3 provides a legal jurisdictional basis for proceedings to be brought before it. Once the matter has been referred to the ICJ, it will be up to the Court to assess whether it is has the appropriate jurisdiction. Several scenarios are then possible. The ICJ may refuse to hear the matter on the grounds of the principle of *res judicata* if, after examining the application, it concludes that the case has already been decided by a regional court.

If, however, the regional courts have declared themselves incompetent or the application inadmissible, the ICJ could decide to exercise its jurisdiction. In applying its jurisdiction to define the subject matter of the dispute,[241] the Court could also declare that it has jurisdiction if it considers that the subject matter of the dispute before it has not been addressed by the regional mechanisms.[242] Article 13.3 of the Volta Basin Authority Convention therefore offers a more interesting alternative for dispute settlement than that proposed by agreements which limit the jurisdiction of dispute settlements to African judicial bodies.[243] It anticipates that there is a risk that dispute settlement within these regional bodies may not always succeed and thus ensures a peaceful alternative to achieve a settlement. This strengthens the mechanics available for the peaceful resolution of the dispute.

The treaty provisions that provide recourse to a permanent court vary with respect to the basis of the court's jurisdiction over contentious matters. Global water conventions, namely the Water Convention[244] and the Watercourses Convention,[245] both include an optional ICJ compulsory jurisdiction clause whereby a party may recognize the jurisdiction of the ICJ as a compulsory means of dispute settlement between it and any other party to the instrument that makes a similar declaration. African basin treaties do not tend to follow

---

241 ICJ, Nuclear Tests Case (Australia v. France), Judgment, 20 December 1974, at 262, para 29; ICJ, Nuclear Tests Case (New Zealand v. France), Judgment, 20 December 1974, at 466, para 30.

242 Compare in this sense with the following ICJ case, Obligation to Negotiate Access to the Pacific Ocean (Bolivia v. Chile), Preliminary Objection, Judgment, 24 September 2015.

243 See, for example, the Orange-Senqu River Commission Agreement, *supra* note 8, Arts 8.2 and 8.3, and the Limpopo River Commission Agreement, *supra* note 18, Art. 9.2, where the Southern African Development Community Tribunal intervenes as a last resort. See also Articles 46.2 and 46.3 of the Lake Victoria Basin Protocol, *supra* note 11, where the East African Court of Justice intervenes as a last resort.

244 Water Convention, *supra* note 27, Art. 22.2.

245 Watercourses Convention, *supra* note 227, Art. 33.10.

this approach and instead follow the more classic principle of the optional jurisdiction of the judicial body, which implies, in each case, the conclusion of a compromise between the parties to the dispute.[246]

A compulsory jurisdiction clause can be read into treaties where they are silent on such a clause, but make direct reference to the ICJ. This is also the case where treaties make reference to regional tribunals, such as the Agreement for the Establishment of the Orange-Senqu River Commission:

> If the Parties to the dispute have not arrived at a settlement through the means provided for in sub Article 8.1, the dispute may, unless the Parties agree otherwise, be brought before the Tribunal established in terms of Article 16(1) of the Treaty of the Southern African Development Community of 1992, in accordance with the rules and procedures applicable with regard to the function of such Tribunal.[247]

A similar provision is contained in the Agreement on the Establishment of the Limpopo Watercourse Commission[248] and the Lake Victoria Basin Protocol.[249] However, the jurisdiction clause adopted by the Agreement on the Establishment of the Zambezi Watercourse Commission is subject to a *sui generis* formulation. Indeed, Article 21.3 of this Agreement states:

> If the parties to the dispute have not arrived at a settlement through the means provided for in paragraphs (1) and (2) of this Article [by way of diplomatic dispute settlement], the dispute may, unless the parties to the dispute agree on another means of settlement, be brought before the

246 This is the case, for example, of the water charters in Africa. This reading can be deduced from the very general and vague wording of the unique provisions concerning the referral to the ICJ: Senegal River Water Charter, *supra* note 84, Art. 30: 'Any dispute which may arise between the signatory parties concerning the interpretation or application of this Charter, its amendments or annexes, shall be resolved by conciliation and mediation ... As a last resort the International Court of Justice shall be seized'; Niger Basin Water Charter, *supra* note 97, Art. 31: 'In the absence of a satisfactory solution at this stage, the parties to the dispute shall first refer the matter to the African Union Conciliation Commission, before any referral to the International Court of Justice'; Lake Chad Basin Water Charter, *supra* note 100, Art. 89: 'If all the aforementioned dispute resolution mechanisms fail, the States concerned in the dispute shall bring the case for arbitration or judicial dispute resolution by the International Court of Justice'.

247 Orange-Senqu River Commission Agreement, *supra* note 8, Art. 8.2.

248 Limpopo River Commission Agreement, *supra* note 18, Art. 9.2.

249 See Article 46. 2 of the Lake Victoria Basin Protocol, *supra* note 11, where reference is instead made to the East African Court of Justice.

> Tribunal by the way of an agreement between Member States which are parties to the dispute or by the way of a reasoned and documented petition on the part of one or more of the parties to the dispute.[250]

This provision establishes the dual jurisdiction of the Southern African Development Community Tribunal, which is both optional and compulsory. On the one hand, it provides for a rather ordinary form of optional jurisdiction, requiring the consent of the parties by agreement in order to refer the case to the Tribunal. On the other hand, it establishes an original form of compulsory jurisdiction, triggered by the ability of one or more parties to bring an action before the Tribunal on the basis of a documented petition. This particular approach raises several questions about the nature, form and substance of this 'documented petition' and its 'power' to confer jurisdiction on the Tribunal. These questions remain unanswered for the time being due to lack of practice, but certainly highlight the richness of the dispute settlement procedures offered by basin organizations.

2.2.2 *The Rise of In-House Dispute Settlement in Basin Organizations*

'In-house' dispute settlement (or the internalization of dispute resolution) within a basin organization is the result of the growing recognition of the ability of these institutions to settle disputes between member states themselves. In concrete terms, the basin organization serves as a framework for the settlement procedure. This internalization leads to the confinement of the dispute within the institution and avoids any recourse to a third party to settle a dispute between member states. In this way, the institution contributes to maintaining the spirit of cooperation between states. Moreover, in-house dispute settlement allows the institution to ensure the proper application of its legal instruments by proposing solutions fully in line with the spirit and the letter of the institution's legal framework. This is particularly important for technical disputes such as pollution cases. The intervention of a third party also runs the risk of decisions being technically unsatisfactory for the basin organization. Therefore, before analysing examples of this internalization in practice (b), it is necessary to understand the regime that underpins and is applicable to it (a).

2.2.2.1 The In-House Dispute Settlement Regime

Understanding the regime applicable to 'in-house' dispute settlement requires both the examination of the basis for such internalization and its limits. The

---

250 Zambezi Watercourse Commission Agreement, *supra* note 12, Art. 21.3.

contribution of basin organizations to the settlement of disputes was highlighted by the Watercourses Convention.[251] This contribution is exclusively limited to disputes between member states. The basin organization's capacity generally stems from an express authorization under its constituent charter. This is the case with the Lake Chad Basin Water Charter which states, 'If the parties fail to come to an agreement after negotiation, any party thereto shall bring the case to the Commission, which shall conduct good offices or mediation procedure in attempt to reach a settlement'. Similarly, Article 34.1(a) of the Agreement on the Nile River Basin Cooperative Framework states: 'If the States concerned cannot reach agreement by negotiation requested by one of them, they may jointly seek good offices, or request mediation or conciliation by, the Nile River Basin Commission or other third party'. A similar mandate is included in Articles 29 and 30 of the Niger Basin Water Charter and Article 13.2 of the Volta Basin Authority Convention.

In other cases, the capacity of basin organizations to resolve disputes is less explicit and emerges from practice according to the needs of member states. The OMVS provides a good illustration. Indeed, the various texts of the OMVS do not expressly provide that the OMVS forms part of the dispute settlement procedure framework. Nevertheless, this organization has developed mechanisms that allow states to resolve their disputes within its organizational framework. It is interesting to note that, in practice, at the OMVS, the use of external dispute resolution mechanisms is almost non-existent.[252]

In general, the settlement of disputes between member states involves several parts of the basin organization. The mechanisms adopted call for a 'tiered settlement procedure' within the institution's internal framework.[253] Such a scale is generally limited to a hierarchy of the various diplomatic methods of dispute resolution. Thus, within the framework of the Niger Basin Water Charter, Article 29 provides that 'in the event of a dispute between two or more State Parties concerning the interpretation or application of the present Charter, the Parties shall seek a solution through the good offices of the [Niger Basin] Authority, mediation or conciliation or by any other peaceful means of dispute settlement'. Under Article 30, if these diplomatic processes fail, the dispute will be referred 'to the [Niger Basin Authority's] Permanent Technical Committee, which shall propose a settlement to the Council of Ministers and the Summit of the Heads of State and Government'.[254]

---

251 Watercourses Convention, *supra* note 227, Art. 33.2.

252 Samboly Ba & Mbengue, *supra* note 215, at 322.

253 Kamto, *supra* note 19, at 907.

254 See also Niger Basin Appendix on Environmental Protection, *supra* note 103, Art. 221.

These particular developments are indicative of a strong willingness to achieve an internal resolution of a dispute within the basin organization. However, there are limitations to this internalization effort. Indeed, this trend towards in-house dispute settlement raises the question of the relationship between the in-house settlement of disputes by basin organizations and the recourse to external third parties.

The ICJ had to rule on this aspect in the case concerning the *Land and Maritime Boundary between Cameroon and Nigeria*. In this case, proceedings were instituted with the Court by Cameroon on 29 March 1994 on the question of sovereignty over the Bakassi peninsula and the delimitation of the maritime boundary in the Gulf of Guinea. Further to an additional application on 6 June 1994, the subject of the dispute was extended to encompass the question of sovereignty over parcels of territory in the Lake Chad area and the territorial boundary from the lake to the sea. Within the deadline for filing the Counter-Memorial, Nigeria filed eight preliminary objections. Of these objections, the third asserted the Court's lack of jurisdiction on the grounds that boundary disputes in the Lake Chad region fell within the exclusive jurisdiction of the Lake Chad Basin Commission.[255] In support of this argument, Nigeria invoked both the treaty texts governing the 1964 Statute of the Lake Chad Basin Commission (Lake Chad Statute) and the practice of member states.[256] Article 9(g) of the Lake Chad Statute gives the Commission the power to 'examine complaints and contribute to the resolution of differences'. In addition, Nigeria argued that the 'procedures for settlement by the Commission are binding upon the Parties' and that Cameroon could therefore not subsequently refer the matter to the Court on the basis of Article 36.2 of the Lake Chad Statute.

The exclusive jurisdiction of the Lake Chad Basin Commission was challenged by Cameroon.[257] In particular, Cameroon argued that 'no provision of the Statute of the Lake Chad Basin Commission establishes in favour of that international organization any exclusive competence in relation to boundary delimitation' and that 'no such exclusive jurisdiction can be inferred from the conduct of member States'.[258] The ICJ also rejected this claim of exclusive jurisdiction of the Lake Chad Basin Commission on the ground that no such rule was reflected in the Lake Chad Statute. Thus, while recognizing that basin

255 ICJ, Land and Maritime Boundary between Cameroon and Nigeria, Preliminary Objections, Judgment, 11 June 1998, at 304, para 61.

256 *Id*, para 62.

257 *Id*, para 63.

258 *Id*.

organizations may be equipped with dispute settlement procedures, the Court considered that the existence of such procedures 'for regional negotiation cannot prevent the Court from exercising the functions conferred upon it by the Charter and the Statute'.[259] With this decision, the Court underlined the importance of taking into account the content of each water agreement to assess the extent of the internalization of the dispute within the basin organization.

The Revised Convention establishing the Niger Basin Authority of 1987 is a very rare case of the internalization of dispute settlement exclusively within the basin organization's framework. Indeed, Article 20 of this Convention provides that disputes that may arise between member states should be settled by direct negotiations and, failing that, they should be brought by one of the parties before the Summit of the Heads of State and Government, the NBA's supreme policy and decision-making body, which must make the final decision. As Amidou Garané has correctly pointed out, 'although one of the main missions of a basin organization is conflict prevention and resolution, some disputes may not always be resolved within the institution and will require diplomatic settlement means involving third parties or even judicial means'.[260] In practice, changes in subsequent NBA instruments reflect this view. For example, in the Niger Basin Water Charter, dispute settlement usually carried out in-house can, in the event of persistent deadlock, be outsourced to the Conciliation Commission of the African Union as a first step and the ICJ as a last resort.[261]

This complementarity between the institution's internal and external settlement procedures is the result of consistent practice. For instance, in the Treaty relating to the Boundary Waters and Questions Arising Along the Border between the United States and Canada, an arbitral tribunal may be constituted when the 'Commission is equally divided or otherwise unable to render a decision or finding as to any questions or matters so referred [to it]'.[262] In addition, when the parties are unable to settle their dispute within the framework of the Permanent Indus Commission, the Indus Waters Treaty provides for, in certain

259 *Id*, at 307, para 68.

260 See Garané, *supra* note 46, at 139, unofficial translation: '*bien que l'une des missions principales d'une organisation de bassin soit la prévention et le règlement des conflits, certains différends ne pourront pas toujours être résolus au sein de l'institution et nécessiteront des modes de règlement diplomatique faisant intervenir des tiers, voire des modes juridictionnels*'.

261 Niger Basin Water Charter, *supra* note 97, Art. 31.

262 Treaty relating to the Boundary Waters and Questions Arising along the Border between the United States and Canada (1909), Art. X.

cases, the intervention of a neutral expert[263] and, in other cases, recourse to arbitration. For disputes arising on the Uruguay River, the ICJ may be called upon to intervene when 'it has not been possible [by the parties] to settle the dispute within 180 days following the notification referred to in article 59' and the dispute 'cannot be settled by direct negotiations'.[264]

Although basin organizations are ideal frameworks for member states to resolve their differences, the practice of not reserving exclusive dispute settlement to such institutions tends to be established. Therefore, although there is a growing trend of basin organizations providing in-house dispute settlement, this does not constitute a substitute for dispute settlement mechanisms external to the organization.

2.2.2.2 Examples of In-House Dispute Settlement

Basin organizations generally rely on traditional dispute resolution mechanisms to resolve disputes between member states. The internalization of dispute settlement is reflected by the contribution of basin organizations to the diplomatic settlement of disputes between member states. Diplomatic settlement is the principal form of involvement by basin organizations in the settlement of disputes between member states. Such involvement can take both informal and formal forms of intervention.

As an informal intervention, basin organizations are generally called upon to facilitate negotiations between the parties to the dispute. This role can be provided for, as highlighted above, in the basin organization's legal instruments. In such cases, the institution is given the mandate to provide good offices or mediation between the state parties to the dispute.[265] But in other cases, this role is implied in practice. In fact, the various forums set up in these organizations are ideal frameworks for the resolution of disputes as they promote the maintenance and holding of regular dialogue between the parties, which can lead to negotiated solutions. By offering these forums to the parties to the dispute, basin organizations may be called upon to intervene in the resolution of disputes between member states.

The role of the OMVS in the dispute over the 'fossil valleys' between Senegal and Mauritania provides a good example of such an intervention. Although this dispute was not in relation to water quality issues, it highlights the contribution

263 Treaty between the Government of India and the Government of Pakistan concerning the Most Complete and Satisfactory Utilisation of the Waters of the Indus System of Rivers (1960), Art. IX. 2(1) and 2(5).

264 Statute of the River Uruguay, *supra* note 178, Art. 60.

265 See, for example, Niger Basin Water Charter, *supra* note 97, Art. 29; Lake Chad Basin Water Charter, *supra* note 100, Art. 87.

of basin organizations to the settlement of disputes between member states. The dispute concerned Senegal's plan between April and May 2001 to use the surplus of the Senegal River to revitalize the dry valleys of the Ferlo, Sine and Saloum rivers.[266] Mauritania denounced the project as being contrary to the 1972 Convention on the Status of Senegal River and forced Senegal to suspend its implementation in order to conduct studies that could demonstrate the project's compatibility with the Convention. Senegal finally put the project on hold. Here, the OMVS contributed to the resolution of the dispute through its good offices.[267]

A basin organization's intervention can in some cases be more formal, as revealed by the *sui generis* mechanism provided for in Article 30 of the Niger Basin Water Charter. This Article provides for recourse to a particular body, the Permanent Technical Committee, an advisory body to the Executive Secretariat of the NBA.[268] Article 30 states:

> If no solution has been found on completion of the good offices, mediation and conciliation procedures, the dispute shall be submitted to the Permanent Technical Committee, which shall propose a settlement to the Council of Ministers and the Summit of Heads of State and Government after six (6) months from the time the Executive Secretariat requested it to propose a settlement.

There are three points about this provision that merit discussion. First, the referral to the Permanent Technical Committee comes after the initial attempts to resolve the dispute diplomatically. The Charter's provision on amicable settlement (Article 29), refers to the parties seeking a settlement 'by the good offices of the Authority, mediation or conciliation, or any other peaceful means of dispute settlement'. However, it is unclear from this provision whether the dispute settlement methods it mentions (apart from good offices) must be solely exercised within the organization's framework, or whether there can be third party involvement. In the case that third parties are allowed to intervene, the procedures provided by Articles 29 and 30 produce a real web of internal and external dispute settlement mechanisms, with 'to-ing and fro-ing' between them. In fact, this situation has the potential to impact upon the effectiveness

266 See Samboly Ba & Mbengue, *supra* note 215, at 322–323; A. Auclair & F. Lasserre, '*Aménagements, politiques et conflits sur l'eau en Afrique de l'Ouest*', VertigO—la revue électronique en sciences de l'environnement (2013), http://vertigo.revues.org/13994 (accessed 23 January 2020).

267 See Samboly Ba & Mbengue, *supra* note 215, at 322–323.

268 See Niger Basin Water Charter, *supra* note 97, Arts 17, 30.

of the dispute resolution process. This is probably why the Appendix to the Niger Basin Water Charter provides a more coherent and precise clarification that recourse to third parties will only take place in the case of a failure of the Permanent Technical Committee's settlement proposals.[269]

Second, the referral to the Permanent Technical Committee is not due to the initiative of the state parties to the dispute, but due to that of the Executive Secretariat. However, in light of the fact that the Permanent Technical Committee is an advisory body to the Executive Secretary, it is in reality the Executive Secretary that is involved in the settlement of the dispute through its Committee. This approach is unique as it highlights the ability of an implementing body to take the initiative in resolving disputes between member states, a function generally reserved for political bodies. However, the ability to do this is limited. In fact, this links us to the third point: the Permanent Technical Committee does not take any decisions against the disputing parties, but instead makes a settlement proposal to the institution's overarching political bodies. In this internal dispute settlement procedure, it is therefore the NBA's political bodies that ultimately take the decision. It must be noted, however, that the provision does not specify the legal consequences that flow from the settlement proposal.

The Permanent Technical Committee's dispute settlement mechanism is similar to mediation proceedings whose initiation is outside the control of the parties to the dispute. However, the parties retain their freedom of consent by having the ability to accept or not accept the proposed solution. By not involving the parties in its initiation, this procedure is intended to be a voluntary and proactive way for the basin organization to achieve a resolution to the dispute. The mobilization of the majority of the institution's organs reflects a real concern in maintaining a cooperative environment between the states riparian to the Niger River. This concern can in some cases result in the exercise of quasi-jurisdictional functions by the basin organization.

Conclusion

The review of the contribution of African basin organizations to the formation of pollution control standards highlights the central role played by these

269 Article 221 of the Niger Basin Appendix on Environmental Protection, *supra* note 103, states: 'In case of failure of the Permanent Technical Committee, States Parties shall have recourse to good offices, mediation or conciliation by third parties, in accordance with the principle of peaceful settlement of disputes'.

institutions in the development of such standards both quantitative and qualitative. In quantitative terms, it can be observed that, as forums for facilitating and assisting member states toward cooperation, basin organizations in Africa encourage riparian states to engage in a permanent and continuous dialogue on the necessary measures to be adopted to protect water resources. In this way, they promote the regular formulation of standards to control transboundary freshwater pollution through their standard setting activities. Whilst recommendations remain their most commonly used tool, conventional treaty methods are increasingly used in some basins. The water charters are a good illustration of this. Through them, basin organizations can promote the sustainable management and protection of water resources by taking into account the universal standards and principles codified in the United Nations global conventions on water, namely the Watercourses Convention and the Water Convention. Moreover, through these water charters, basin organizations are moving away from the traditional approach of cooperation (which tends to focus only on the use of the resource) to integration of the requirements for protecting the water resource and its ecosystem. The use of normative tools of a mandatory nature, such as appendices and technical regulations, as well as normative tools of a recommendatory nature, highlights the variety of normative methods used by these institutions to prevent and control pollution. This allows basin organizations' to use the most suitable normative method according to the specific circumstances and thus frame and guide the behaviour of actors that are most likely to pollute the resource. This multiplication and diversification of normative powers contributes to a better protection of water resources.

In qualitative terms, there is a trend towards refining the content of pollution control standards. This development stems from the increased participation of non-state actors in the formation of standards to protect transboundary water resources from pollution. This participation contributes both to the legitimacy and effectiveness of the measures adopted by basin organizations, as the measures are more likely to be supported by the surrounding riparian population. The dynamism of basin organizations in this respect emphasizes a marked transition in the role of basin organizations from a purely accompanying role for riparian states to that of a central body and mechanism in the formation of pollution control standards.

However, this enhancement to the substance of pollution control standards could be further strengthened. Firstly, in terms of the involvement of non-state actors, the mechanisms and tools in place that allow for participation are still only consultative in scope and therefore limit the full potential impact of non-state actors. Public participation in African basin organizations thus remains a work in progress. An important challenge remains for these bodies to develop mechanisms to better integrate, and give full effect to, the inputs from all actors working to protect water, including representatives of civil society and experts in water science (hydrology, chemistry, etc.), as well as all those in the community who depend on the water resource for their basic needs.

Secondly, the efficiency and effectiveness of standards could be further enhanced by viewing non-state actors as recipients of the normative measures issued by basin organizations. Currently, the main beneficiaries of a basin organization's standard setting powers are the member states that have set them up and delegated the necessary powers to them. In light of the significant role private sector and individual communities play in creating water pollution, basin organizations could adopt a preventive approach that supports state action and transcends any state barriers by directly enacting norms of behaviour for private industry and individuals. The power to issue such norms could be expressly set out in the constituent instruments of the organization. Therefore, it would not be a general but a specialized competence of the organization in support of the primary action of the state. This could take, for example, the form of recommendations of good practice to be applied in specific areas identified as sources of pollution which have an impact on shared water resources. Although the implementation of such measures at the national level would remain the responsibility of states, basin organizations could facilitate implementation through raising awareness in, and supporting the activities of, local communities, as currently practiced in several African basins.

Basin organizations in Africa have made a significant contribution due to their increased involvement in the implementation of standards for the prevention of freshwater pollution. This is indicative of their supervisory role in ensuring respect for the law. The development of the mandate of basin organizations can, first of all, be observed through the extension of the scope of their control and monitoring activities. This extension is of a material nature and is demonstrated by basin organizations controlling and monitoring the standards they have issued. Basin organizations therefore have *a posteriori* control over the application of pollution control standards through procedures that require ongoing monitoring on a regular basis. This is the case, for example, with the reporting procedure at the Lake Tanganyika Authority or the Lake Victoria Basin Commission. Basin organizations can also have a form of *a priori* control over the implementation of pollution control standards by using certain monitoring techniques in specific contexts, such as the assent or prior information procedures, as seen in the practice of the Lake Chad Basin Commission. The power to supervise and monitor the implementation of the standards developed by basin organizations promotes the better protection of international fresh water. In fact, a well-executed evaluation of the implementation of standards can go on to encourage the adoption of complementary measures. This highlights the preventative nature and value of monitoring and control activities in the protection of transboundary fresh waters.

Another aspect to note is that through their monitoring and control functions, basin organizations are also able to monitor the compliance with standards enacted under other legal frameworks. Indeed, the standards incorporated in basin regimes generally stem from international conventions and regulations. This is the case at the regional level, with instruments adopted within regional economic areas such as the Southern African Development Community, the Economic Community of Central African States and the Economic Community of Western African States. This is also true at the international level with, for example, the water conventions adopted within the United Nations system, namely the Watercourses Convention and the Water Convention, or multilateral environmental conventions such as the Convention on Biological Diversity (1992) and the Ramsar Convention on Wetlands of International Importance (1971). By relying on such instruments to develop their own legal regime, basin organizations, through their monitoring and control powers, participate in the enforcement of these universally accepted norms and standards. As a result, basin organizations are an important tool in supporting states compliance with their international obligations and thus provide a framework to help achieve consistency across the various international obligations.

The development of basin organizations' dispute resolution mandate is a key aspect of their contribution to the protection of water resources. This can be observed by the rise of 'in-house' dispute settlement within basin organizations. This internalization reflects a real focus to preserve a climate of close cooperation between riparian states and hence further enhance their role as providers of an accessible framework for cooperation. To that end, basin organizations are involved in all aspects of dispute management, whether it is a matter of preventing disputes or resolving them peacefully. They have a wide range of means at their disposal to resolve disputes within their frameworks. However, practice indicates that the involvement of basin organizations is currently limited to disputes between states. Moreover, the contribution of basin organizations to the settlement of disputes is generally showcased via diplomatic means. Such dispute settlement means are unlikely to undermine the confidence of riparian states in basin organizations. This in turn enables them to play a full role as a preferred forum for cooperation.

This increasing internalization of dispute settlement does not, however, preclude the possibility of dispute settlement taking place outside of basin organizations. In African practice, the regionalization of judicial settlement is the norm, and is evidenced by the primacy accorded to the referral to regional judicial mechanisms. But, as observed, the instruments that provide for the possibility of a referral as a last resort to a universal jurisdiction, such as the International Court of Justice, offer a valuable alternative that improves the prospect of the peaceful settlement of disputes. Indeed, it anticipates the potential risk of failure to settle a dispute before regional bodies and therefore ensures the existence of a peaceful alternative settlement framework. In a similar manner, the option of resorting, if necessary, to the good offices of organizations operating on a global scale, such as the Implementation Committee of the Water Convention, also offers a non-judicial dispute mechanism that helps to strengthen the overall dispute settlement framework.

From this study, it is clear that over time, the protection of water resources and their ecosystems has become a key focus of basin organizations in Africa. The development, adoption and implementation of pollution control standards by basin organizations have widened the remit and greatly strengthened the role of these institutions. As such, basin organizations have become central actors in the domain of African regional law for the protection of freshwater resources.

Acknowledgement

I would like to express my sincere thanks to Dr. Salman M. A. Salman and Professor Laurence Boisson de Chazournes for their continued support and encouragement throughout the writing of this monograph. My thanks and appreciation are also due to the anonymous reviewers, as well as the members of the Editorial Board of *Brill Research Perspectives in International Water Law*, for overseeing the review process, and for the helpful and constructive comments on the monograph.

Author Biography

Dr. Komlan Sangbana serves as a Legal Officer with the Secretariat of the Convention on Protection and Use of Transboundary Watercourses and International Lakes (UNECE). Since 2009, he has been a Research Fellow with the Platform for International Water Law (University of Geneva School of Law). Previously he worked at the University of Geneva as a Scientific Collaborator where he developed and coordinated a massive open online course on International Water Law, and at the Geneva Water Hub as a Scientific Officer on projects related to the governance of transboundary basins in Africa and Europe. Dr. Sangbana holds a postgraduate degree in Public Law from the University of Lomé (Togo) and a Doctorate in International Law from the University of Geneva (Switzerland). He has also been a visiting scholar (Postdoctorate) to the Faculty of Law of the University of Edinburgh (United Kingdom).

Bibliography

Adam, H. T., *Les organismes internationaux spécialisés. Contribution à la théorie générale des établissements publics internationaux* (Paris: Librairie Générale de Droit et de Jurisprudence, 1957).

Auclair, A. & F. Lasserre, *'Aménagements, politiques et conflits sur l'eau en Afrique de l'Ouest'*, VertigO—la revue électronique en sciences de l'environnement (2013), http://vertigo.revues.org/13994.

Bedredine, F. & G. Fabre, *'Examples of concerted and supportive management of a shared river basin (Guinea, Mali, Mauritania, Senegal)'*, paper presented at the International Network of Basin Organizations, 10th World General Assembly (2010).

Boisson de Chazournes, L. & M. Tignino M., *'Le règlement des différends internationaux relatifs à l'eau'*, in Conseil d'État, *L'eau et son droit. Etudes et documents du Conseil d'État* (Paris: La documentation française, 2010) 489–514.

Boisson de Chazournes, L., *Fresh Water in International Law* (Oxford: Oxford University Press, 2013).

Boisson de Chazournes, L., *'Organismes et commissions de bassins: Aspects de coopération régionale et règlement des différends'*, in M. Kamga & M. M. Mbengue (eds), *L'Afrique et le droit international: Variations sur l'organisation internationale, Liber Amicorum en l'honneur de Raymond Ranjeva* (Pedone, 2013), 435–444.

Boisson de Chazournes, L., M. Kohen & J. E. Viñuales, (eds), *Diplomatic and Judicial Means of Dispute Settlement* (Leiden: Martinus Nijhoff, 2013).

Boisson de Chazournes, L., & Mbengue M. M., 'Suivi et contrôle', in E. Lagrange & J.-M. Sorel, *Traité de droit des organisations internationales* (Paris: Librairie Générale de Droit et de Jurisprudence, 2013) 402–433.

Brachet C. & R. Dessouassi, *A Shared Vision for the Niger Basin* (Niamey; Niger Basin Authority, 2008).

Brown Weiss, E., *International Law in a Water-Scarce World* (Leiden/Boston: Brill, 2013).

Caflisch, L, *'Règles générales du droit des cours d'eau internationaux'*, in L. Caflisch & G. Tunkin, (eds), *Recueil des cours/Académie de droit international de La Haye* (1989) 9–225.

Cahin, G., '*La variété des fonctions imparties aux organisations internationales*', in E. Lagrange & J.-M. Sorel, (eds), *Traité de droit des organisations internationales* (Paris: Librairie Générale de Droit et de Jurisprudence, 2013) 671–704.

Charpentier, J., '*Le contrôle par les organisations internationales de l'exécution des obligations des États*', 4:182, Recueil des Cours, Académie de Droit International (1983) 143–246.

Collier, J. & A. V. Lowe, *The Settlement of Disputes in International Law* (Oxford University Press, 1999).

Daillier, P., M. Forteau & A. Pellet, *Droit international public* (8th edition, Paris: Librairie Générale de Droit et de Jurisprudence, 2009).

Dessouassi, R. Y., '*État du processus de gestion intégrée des ressources en eau dans le Bassin du Niger: Expériences de l'implication des acteurs non étatiques et de la prévention des conflits entre usagers de ressources*', in M. Tignino & K. Sangbana, (eds), *Public Participation and Water Resources Management: Where Do We Stand in International Law?* (Paris: UNESCO-IHP, 2015) 69–76.

De Stefano, L., & G. Schmidt, '*Public Participation and Water Management in the European Union: Experiences and Lessons Learned*', in B. Cosens, (ed), *The Columbia River Treaty Revisited: Transboundary River Governance in the Face of Uncertainty* (Corvallis: Oregon State University Press, 2012), 383–397.

Dombrowsky, I., *Conflict, Cooperation, and Institutions in International Water Management: An Economic Analysis* (Cheltenham: Edward Elgar, 2007).

Dominicé, C., '*Valeur et autorité des actes des organisations internationales*', in R.-J. Dupuy, (ed), *Manuel sur les organisations internationales/A Handbook on International Organizations* (2nd edition, Dordrecht: Martinus Nijhoff, 1998) 441–484.

Dupuy, P. M., & Y. Kerbrat, *Droit international public* (12th edition, Dalloz, 2014).

Dupuy, R.-J., '*État et organisation internationale*', in R.-J. Dupuy, (ed), *Manuel sur les organisations internationals/A Handbook on International Organizations* (2nd edition, Dordrecht: Martinus Nijhoff, 1998) 11–30.

Elias, T. O., '*The Commission of Mediation, Conciliation and Arbitration of the Organization of African Unity*', 41, British Yearbook of International Law (1964) 336–354.

Garané, A., *Le cadre juridique international du bassin de la Volta* (Gland: IUCN, 2009).

Godana, B. A., *Africa's Shared Water Resources: Legal and Institutional Aspects of the Nile, Niger and Senegal River Systems* (London: Frances Pinter, 1985).

Higgins, R., '*The Role of Resolutions of International Organizations in the Process of Creating Norms in the International System*', in W. E. Butler, (ed), *International Law and the International System* (Dordrecht: Martinus Nijhoff, 1987) 21–39.

International Network of Basin Organizations et al, *The Handbook for Integrated Water Resources Management in Transboundary Basins of Rivers, Lakes and Aquifers* (INBO and GWP, 2012).

Jacob, P., '*La mise en œuvre des normes et opérations de l'organisation internationale*', in E. Lagrange & J.-M. Sorel, (eds), *Traité de droit des organisations internationales* (Paris: Librairie Générale de Droit et de Jurisprudence, 2013) 861–890.

Kamto, M., '*Le droit international des ressources en eau continentales africaines*', 36:1, Annuaire français de droit international (1990) 843–911.

Krchnak, K. M., '*Improving Water Governance Through Increased Public Access to Information and Participation*', 5:1, Sustainable Development Law and Policy (2005) 34–39.

Lammers, J. G., '*The Interplay between the UN Watercourses Convention and the UNECE Convention on the Protection and Use of Transboundary Watercourses and International Lakes*', in L. Boisson de Chazournes et al(eds.), *The UN Convention on the Law of the Non-Navigational Uses of International Watercourse: A Commentary* (Oxford: Oxford University Press, 2018) 423–424.

Mbengue, M. M., '*Technique de l'opting out: acceptation par les États des normes techniques internationales*', in E. Brosset & E. Truilhé-Marengo, (eds), *Les enjeux de la normalisation technique internationale: Entre environnement, santé et commerce international* (Aix-en-Provence/Paris: CERIC/La documentation française, 2006), 121–152.

Mbengue, M. M., '*Les Chartes de l'eau: Vers une nouvelle conception de la gestion des ressources en eau partagées en Afrique?*', in M. Kamga & M. M. Mbengue, (eds), *L'Afrique et le droit international: Variations sur l'organisation internationale, Liber Amicorum en l'honneur de Raymond Ranjeva* (Paris: Pedone, 2013) 219–231.

McCaffrey, S. C., *The Law of International Watercourses* (Oxford: Oxford University Press, 2019).

Merle, M., '*Le pouvoir réglementaire des institutions internationales*', 4, Annuaire français de droit international (1958) 341–360.

Merle, M., '*Le contrôle exercé par les organisations internationales sur les activités des États membres*', 5, Annuaire français de droit international (1959) 411–431.

Merrills, J. G., *International Dispute Settlement* (Cambridge: Cambridge University Press, 2011).

Mubiala, M., '*Le régionalisme africain en droit international fluvial*', 6, African Journal of International and Comparative Law (1994) 449–471.

Ngaïde, M., '*La contribution de l'Afrique à la gestion des ressources en eau transfrontalières: L'exemple la Charte de l'eau du Bassin du Niger*', 66, Revue juridique et politique des états francophones (2012) 263–316.

Niger Basin Authority, *Elaboration du plan d'action de développement durable du bassin du Niger: Phase II: Schéma directeur d'aménagement et de gestion* (Niamey: NBA, 2007).

Razzaque J., '*Public Participation in Water Governance*', in J. W. Dellapenna & J. Gupta, (eds), *The Evolution of the Law and Politics of Water* (Dordrecht: Springer, 2009) 353–371.

Ruiz Fabri, H., L. A. Sicilianos & J.-M. Sorel, *L'effectivité des organisations internationales: mécanismes de suivi et de contrôle* (Paris: Pedone, 2000).

Ryabtsev, A. D., '*On Public Participation in Water Resources Management*', in P. Wouters, V. Dukhovny & A. Allan, (eds), *Implementing Integrated Water Resources Management in Central Asia* (Dordrecht: Springer, 2007) 89–94.

Sachariew, K., '*Promoting Compliance with International Environmental Legal Standards: Reflections on Monitoring and Reporting Mechanisms*', 2, Yearbook of International Environmental Law (1991) 31–52.

Salman, S. M. A., '*Legal Regime for the Use and Protection of International Watercourse in the Southern African Region: Evolution and Context*', 41, Natural Resources Journal (2001) 981–1022.

Salman, S. M. A., '*The Nile Basin Cooperative Framework Agreement: A Peacefully Unfolding African Spring?*', 31:1 Water International (2013) 17–29.

Salman, S. M. A., '*The Nile River Basin and its Changing Legal Contours*', in S. C. McCaffrey, C. Leb & R. T. Denoon, (eds), *Research Handbook on International Water Law* (Cheltenham: Edward Elgar, 2019) 379–396.

Salmon, J., *Dictionnaire de droit international public* (Brussels: Bruylant, 2001).

Samboly Ba, A., & M. M. Mbengue, '*Le régime juridique du fleuve Sénégal: Aspect du droit des cours d'eau dans un contexte régional*', 12, African Yearbook of International Law (2006) 309–347.

Sangbana, K., '*La gestion intégrée des ressources en eaux partagées et les organismes de bassin en Afrique: le cas de l'Autorité du Bassin du Niger et de l'Autorité de la Volta*', in *Actes du colloque de la Société française pour le droit international, L'eau en droit international* (Paris: Pedone, 2011) 235–244.

Sangbana, K., '*The Role of Non-State Actors in the Development and Implementation of International Water Law*', in A. Rieu-Clarke, A. Allan, & S. Hendry, (eds), *Routledge Handbook of Water Law and Policy* (Abingdon: Routledge, 2017) 287–296.

Schermers, H. G., & N. M. Blokker, *International Institutional Law* (5th edition, Leiden/Boston: Martinus Nijhoff, 2011).

Sohnle, J., *Le droit international des ressources en eau douce: solidarité contre souveraineté* (Paris: La documentation française, 2002).

Southern African Development Community, *Guidelines for Strengthening River Basin Organisations: Environmental Management* (Gaborone: SADC Secretariat, 2010).

Southern African Development Community, *Guidelines for Strengthening River Basin Organisations. Stakeholder Participation* (Gaborone: SADC Secretariat, 2010).

Sow, M., & B. Touré, *État des lieux du cadre juridique et institutionnel dans la région d'intervention en Mauritanie* (OMVS/GEF/BFS, 2008).

Tanzi, A., '*The UN Convention on International Watercourses as a Framework for the Avoidance and Settlement of Water Law Disputes*', 11:3, Leiden Journal of International Law (1998) 441–472.

Tanzi, A., & C. Contartese, '*Dispute Prevention, Dispute Settlement and Implementation Facilitation in International Water Law: The Added Value of the Establishment of an Implementation Mechanism Under the Water Convention*', in A. Tanzi et al (eds), *The UNECE Convention on the Protection and Use of Transboundary Watercourses and International Lakes* (Leiden/Boston: Brill/Nijhoff, 2015) 317–329.

Tignino, M., '*Les contours du principe de la participation du public et la protection des ressources en eau transfrontières*', VertigO—la revue électronique en sciences de l'environnement (2010), http://vertigo.revues.org/9750.

Tignino, M. & K. Sangbana, (eds), *Public Participation and Water Resources Management: Where Do We Stand in International Law?* (Paris: UNESCO-IHP, 2015).

Toope S. J., & J. Brunnée, '*Freshwater Regimes: The Mandate of the International Joint Commission*', 15, Arizona Journal of International and Comparative Law (1998) 272–287.

Trombitcaia, I., & S. Koeppel, '*From a Regional towards a Global Instrument: The 2003 Amendment to the UNECE Water Convention*', in A. Tanzi et al (eds), *The UNECE Convention on the Protection and Use of Transboundary Watercourses and International Lakes* (Leiden/Boston: Brill/Nijhoff, 2015) 15–31.

Ulfstein, G., '*Les activités normatives de l'organisation internationale*', in E. Lagrange & J.-M. Sorel, *Traité de droit des organisations internationales* (Paris: Librairie Générale de Droit et de Jurisprudence, 2013), 737–755.

United Nations, *Handbook on the Peaceful Settlement of International Disputes between States* (New York: United Nations, 1992).

United Nations Development Programme & Global Environment Facility, *Protecting International Waters—'Sustaining Livelihoods'* (New York: UNDP/GEF, 2004).

United Nations Economic Commission for Europe, *Guide to Implementing the Water Convention* (New York and Geneva: United Nations, 2013).

United Nations Economic Commission for Europe, *Principles for Effective Joint Bodies for Transboundary Water Cooperation* (New York and Geneva: United Nations, 2018).

UN Water, United Nations Economic Commission for Europe, and United Nations Educational Scientific and Cultural Organization, *Progress on Transboundary Water Cooperation: Global Baseline for SDG Indicator 6.5.2* (Paris: UNESCO, 2018).

Virally, M., '*La valeur juridique des recommandations des organisations internationales*', 2, Annuaire français de droit international (1956) 66–96.

www.ingramcontent.com/pod-product-compliance
Lightning Source LLC
Chambersburg PA
CBHW031333230926
51848CB00001B/209
9789004436619